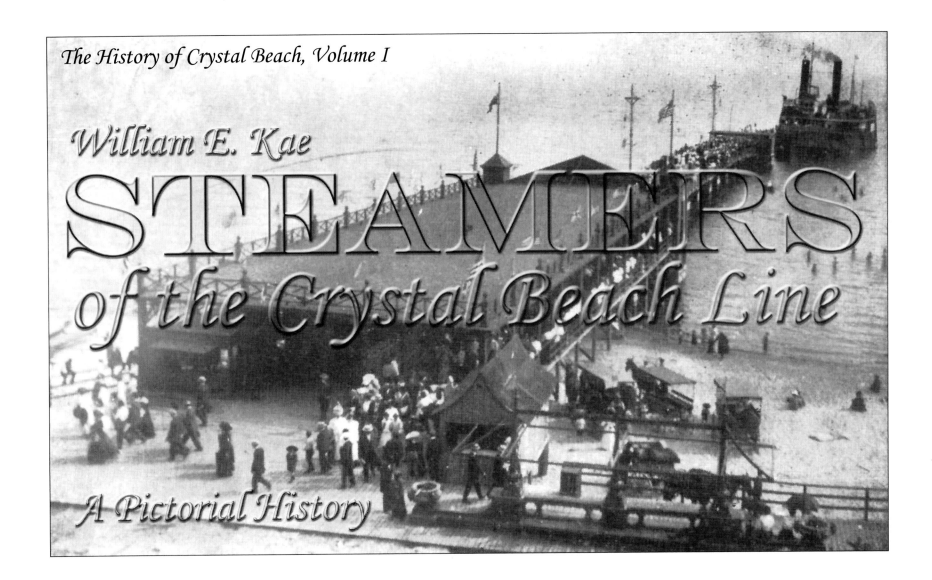

The History of Crystal Beach, Volume I

William E. Kae

STEAMERS
of the Crystal Beach Line

A Pictorial History

STEAMERS *of the Crystal Beach Line*

Published by:

P.O. Box 1155
Buffalo, New York 14201
cyclonebooks@verizon.net

ISBN: 978-0-9796632-0-8

Library of Congress Control Number: 2007903855

Kae, William E., 1959 -
Crystal Beach, Ontario; Buffalo, New York;
The History of Crystal Beach, Volume 1: Steamers of the Crystal Beach Line: A Pictorial History
-1st ed.
216 p. : photos
Includes bibliographical references and index.

Summary: Historical synopsis of the Crystal Beach Line steamers
that sailed between Buffalo, New York and Crystal Beach, Ontario.

Unless specified, all photographs are from the collection of

**The Lower Lakes Marine Historical Society
66 Erie Street
Buffalo, New York 14202**

Note on Americana/Canadiana Blue Print Reproduction: Every effort was made to reproduce the blue prints from the American Ship Building Company with as much clarity as possible, but there were a number of unmitigated factors that prevented reproduction to the author's liking. The images supplied by Bowling Green State University were provided on microfilm and are of excellent quality. Reproduction of the image on microfilm to paper, in essence shrank sections of 3-foot long and longer blue prints to less than eleven inches to fit within the margins of this book. Such a reduction in scale makes the sharpest details impossible to read - particularly the text and lettering. Microfilm to paper printing equipment available to the author added visible "noise" to the hard copy reproduction precipitated by dusty lenses and scratched mirrors. Once on paper, the prints were scanned and the noise removed with imaging software. Most of the text was unintelligible, so it was removed with the visual noise, and recreated using the imaging software. Anyone interested in the availability of obtaining prints or microfilm for their personal use should contact the Historical Collections of the Great Lakes, Bowling Green State University.

Table of Contents

Acknowledgments

Appendix

Bibliography

Index

Acknowledgements

The Canadiana had ceased sailing between Buffalo, New York and Crystal Beach, Ontario five or six years before my first Crystal Beach visit, which is locked away in the recesses of my memory and beyond my ability to recall. In subsequent years, I listened to the recollections of my parents and grandparents of a Crystal Beach that did not resemble the one I had become familiar with. Theirs was a Crystal Beach reached by boat and filled with rides and roller coasters that had ceased operating long before the boat ceased sailing. Their stories seemed to me an incredible fiction, but the concrete pier stretching out into Point Abino Bay like an arthritic finger where the boat docked was the proof that this earlier Crystal Beach did once exist. This pier (that in the 1960s looked as if it had seen better days) and its earlier versions was once Crystal Beach Park's front door. The steamers of the Crystal Beach Line, from 1890 through 1956, delivered more people to this front door than all the buses and cars did after boat service ended. This realization came me during the mid 1990s when I began in-depth research on Crystal Beach.

I was planning to write a comprehensive history of Crystal Beach Park to be contained in one volume. During the initial drafts, Jane Davies, Erin Wilson and Jude Scott of the Fort Erie Historical Museum in Ridgeway, Ontario suggested that a series of stand alone topical volumes would permit more in-depth coverage and photos than a single volume covering all aspects of Crystal Beach history would allow. If I had not followed their suggestion, the subject matter in this volume would appear as an abbreviated chapter in an all-encompassing book.

Development of this volume required more images about the subject than I had earlier acquired. Jack Messmer and the Lower Lakes Marine Historical Society of Buffalo made their entire collection of photos and archival material available to me and continue to support and encourage this project.

It was also a privledge to meet George Rebstock Jr. who generously provided a rare photo portrait of his grandfather, John E. Rebstock, the founder of Crystal Beach.

As this volume was about to go to press, I had the pleasure of meeting Rick Doan who made available photographs from his collection. Rick introduced me to Cathy Herbert and Harvey Holzworth. Cathy and Harvey contributed many rare images. The contributions of Rick, Cathy, and Harvey expanded this volume considerably. To Don Oatman, president of the No. 6 RCAF Dunnville Museum for information on the Harvard Trainer crash not covered in Buffalo newspapers.

Lastly, to my other sets of eyes, Ron Dukam, Keith Hansult, Geraldine Kae, Mary Ann Kae, Alexis Koral, Ed Koral, Jack Messmer and Arlene Swank for review of the drafts, comments and suggestions. -WEK

$\mathcal{D}$edicated to my mother, Geraldine Kae (kneeling), and my
grandmother behind her, Sophie Radominski.
Photo taken at Crystal Beach Park, 1940.

Introduction

The following pages contain historical sketches of a select group of steamboats that sailed the Great Lakes. Distinguishing these steamers from all others is the fact that they sailed between Buffalo, New York and Crystal Beach, Ontario at some point during their existence. While the chronicles are specific to the steamers, they provide a glimpse into a way of life erased by time and technology.

The primary mode of transportation when Crystal Beach opened in 1890 was horse and buggy. Aviation was limited to hot air balloons and used mostly for entertainment. Electricity was more of a scientific curiosity than a practical utility - its widespread use was science fiction fodder. And with regard to today's science fiction classics from the late 19th century, H.G. Wells was a few years away from penning "The Invisible Man," "The Time Machine," and "War of the Worlds."

The Crystal Beach Line (the Line) existed when Buffalo was a major port on the Great Lakes. The Line outlived most of the other passenger ship lines that trains, planes, automobiles and the economies of technology had earlier choked out of existence.

Not only are the steamers of the Crystal Beach Line a distinguished group of vessels, they are also an excellent representative sample of short and medium haul passenger steamers that sailed the Great Lakes with the same relative concentration that today's commercial airliners navigate the sky. Their operational history parallels that of many other steamers.

Along the shores of Lake Erie, and the Niagara and Buffalo Rivers, remnants of Buffalo's former Great Lakes status are easy to find. However, remnants of Buffalo's steamboat passenger lines have disappeared except for two: the Crystal Beach pier that the forces of Lake Erie are slowly erasing, and the Erie Beach pier - abandoned since 1930, is now mostly rubble. Only the Canadiana's propeller and one or two of her bollards and cap-stan set in a monument are all that remain of the Crystal Beach Line. The monument is on display twenty-four hours a day, seven days a week at the Crystal Beach Waterfront Park in Crystal Beach. The City of Buffalo provides the perfect backdrop for the tribute to the Canadiana and a line of steamers that was once so important to both of these locales.

In this photo of Buffalo (circa 1905), the street clearly visible across the Buffalo River is Washington Street. Just to the left of the center of the photo is a tug boat where at its stern is the Main Street dock. Very little in this scene of downtown Buffalo remains in early 21st century Buffalo. Structures in the background that are still standing today are: the 209 foot tower of Erie County Hall (just to the left of center on the horizon) and just in front of it is the steeple of St. Joseph's Cathedral. Just right of the center is the splinter-like steeple of St. Paul's Cathedral. Continuing to the right is the recently completed Ellicott Square Building. Peeking from behind of the wooden grain elevator is the tower of the brand new post office that opened in 1901 - today it is the home of the downtown campus of Erie County Community College.

Dock conditions at the foot of Main Street, circa 1895. The steamer at the extreme left of the photo is the Pearl of the Crystal Beach Line. The Puritan, another steamer of the Line, is just to the left of center of the photo. Steamers immediately at dockside often let passengers cross their decks to reach steamers unable to find docking space. Without this courtesy, steamers would be unable to depart their dockside mooring, held in by steamers needing to dock.

The Crystal Beach Line

CHAPTER 1

Crystal Beach, Ontario was one of a number of resorts on the Niagara Frontier (and one of thousands in North America) that began during an era when very few people had leisure time or disposable income. What little of these commodities people had available to them was spent locally. Long distance travel was an arduous, time consuming, and exhausting undertaking, so even the rich spent a great deal of time and money locally and regionally. Because of the relative immobility of the populace, summer resorts and amusement parks sprouted in and around population centers. In the immediate vicinity of the Niagara Frontier, most of the resorts were on Grand Island, along with a number of "club resorts" that catered to the middle and upper classes.

Crystal Beach became a summer destination for families of all classes. Families with little disposable income scrimped and saved for an entire year just for a day's outing. For others less financially challenged, Crystal Beach became an overnight, weekend or vacation retreat frequented numerous times during the summer. Even Buffalo's wealthy were attracted to Crystal Beach and peaceful Point Abino Bay, many of whom built stately homes along its sandy shores.

The easiest way for U.S. citizens to reach Crystal Beach (and for a very long time, the only way to reach Grand Island) was by steamboat. During the summer months of the late 1800s and early 1900s, steamers clogged the harbor at the Main Street dock in Buffalo, vying for space to collect passengers bound for the summer fun spots.

Within a few years after Crystal Beach opened in mid-July 1890, it became the predominant summer resort on the Niagara Frontier. People flocked to downtown Buffalo then boarded the Main Street trolley that deposited them just north of the dock at the last trolley stop. Because the Crystal Beach Line operators sold tickets without consideration to steamer capacity and departure times, often there were more people wanting to board a steamer than its license permitted it to carry. Many ticketed people had to wait for the next departure or longer, while the area between the trolley stop and the dock became a sea of humanity waiting for a steamer to Crystal Beach.

Island Club, Grand Island, Buffalo, N. Y.

The largest private club in the early 1900s was the Oakfield (below) with over 400 members. The steamer Lorelei brought guests from Buffalo. The club suffered from two fires, and when the membership declined, the property was sold.

A parade of people walk down the Island Club pier on Grand Island (above) from an unseen steamer that had just landed.

Images of the Bedell House on Grand Island

Author's collection.

Author's collection.

The "House" in the pen and ink drawing burned in 1886, and replaced by the one in the lower left image. Above right, the busy Bedell House wharf, and in the lower right, an unidentified steamer (probably the Island Belle or the Osian Bedell). The Bedell House was the most popular of all the resorts on Grand Island and operated as early as 1874 when ferry service began from Bedell House to the foot of Sheridan Drive in the Town of Tonawanda until its final version burned in 1988.

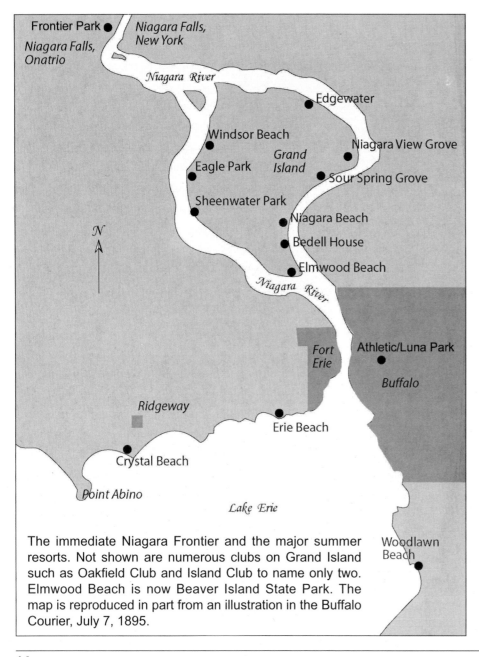

The immediate Niagara Frontier and the major summer resorts. Not shown are numerous clubs on Grand Island such as Oakfield Club and Island Club to name only two. Elmwood Beach is now Beaver Island State Park. The map is reproduced in part from an illustration in the Buffalo Courier, July 7, 1895.

People would stay at the park as long as possible and without harbormasters keeping count of those boarding at the Crystal Beach pier, the last steamers of the evening returning to Buffalo were often filled beyond their licensed capacity.

Steamers were the primary means of transportation to Crystal Beach, but they were not the only means. The ambitious could take their own horse and buggy (and eventually their own automobile) across the Niagara River on one of the ferries that operated between Squaw Island and Fort Erie, then follow approximately 12 miles of bridal paths. Another option was by train that crossed the International Railroad Bridge and stopped at Ridgeway. There, travelers transferred to the Ontario Southern Railway that was one of the earliest monorails. Just slightly more inconvenient, perhaps, was taking a train from Buffalo to Ridgeway, then taking a carriage from Ridgeway to Crystal Beach. Driving to Crystal Beach did not become practical until the completion of the Peace Bridge in 1927 - nearly forty years after Crystal Beach opened.

Taking a steamer was the easiest and most direct way to reach Crystal Beach. It remained popular for many years, proven by the fact that

Gridlock at the ferry dock in Fort Erie. This was one of many ferry landings on the Canadian shore.

Author's collection.

Cars at the Fort Erie ferry landing waiting to be cleared through customs. The ferry Newtown is docked.

At the landing on Squaw Island, cars board a ferry. This service continued after completion of the Peace Bridge, but operating costs and declining patronage would eventually bring it to an end.

the various owners of Crystal Beach Park operated the Crystal Beach Line for over 67 years.

John E. Rebstock, founder of Crystal Beach, leased and operated an armada of steamers through the Crystal Beach Steamboat and Ferry Company (CBSFC) - the company he formed with a number of investors after Crystal Beach's debut season.

The CBSFC leased all but two of the steamers the company operated. The leases were seasonal and the number of steamers available for lease changed annually. Occasionally, steamship owners sold their vessels during the off season to individuals or companies that sailed them for their own transportation needs. In addition, age or accidents precipitated the decommissioning of steamers that wound up abandoned, scrapped, or stripped down to the hull and used as barges. Vessel owners did not necessarily have loyalty to a lessee, and executed leases for idle vessels to the first individual or entity to agree to the lease terms. Therefore, in spring when the CBSFC began their search for steamers, not all of the previous season's ships were available. More often than not, the Crystal Beach Line fleet changed with each season. (See Appendix Table 1.) There were years when the CBSFC could have operated three or more steamers but operated one or two simply because there were no steamers available. Occasionally, CBSFC faced their own advertised season opening without a vessel on the line because the steamer(s) they leased had not yet arrived in Buffalo from its home port. Fortunately, other local steamboat operators assisted the Crystal Beach Line for the short term until their contracted vessels arrived.

It wasn't until the Lake Erie Excursion Company (LEEC), with investments from officers of the Cleveland and Buffalo Transit Company, took controlling interest of Crystal Beach that the annual parade of steamers ended. This company recognized the potential of Crystal Beach to become a major summer amusement resort, but in order to realize the potential, the company needed a reliable steamship line with vessels that could transport thousands at a time.

A DISAPPOINTMENT.

The Steamer Ossifrage Will Not Come to Buffalo After All.

The Crystal Beach Steamboat Company received a dispatch from F. W. Wheeler last evening stating that his excursion steamer Ossifrage would not come to Buffalo, as she was under contract to run elsewhere. Secretary Knight said the Company wired Mr. Wheeler an offer for her services on Friday. He replied that she would leave Bay City for Buffalo that night and the inference of course was that the offer had been accepted.

A private dispatch to the COURIER says that the Ossifrage has been chartered by Mr. Wheeler to Gilman & Barnes of Detroit, to run to their resort on Fighting Island, a few miles below Detroit, until October 1.

The Crystal Beach Company are much displeased over Mr. Wheeler's apparent change of front. They intend to get some other boat if Possible.

Left: Ontario Southern Railway that ran for a short time between Crystal Beach and Ridgeway during the late 1890s.
Above: Reproduced from the Buffalo Courier, July 20, 1891

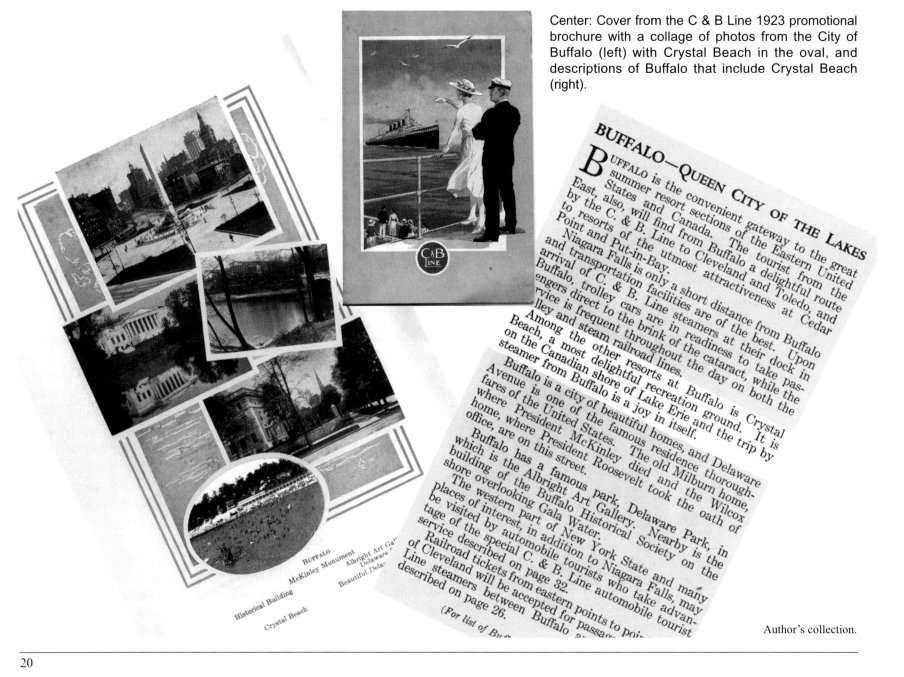

Center: Cover from the C & B Line 1923 promotional brochure with a collage of photos from the City of Buffalo (left) with Crystal Beach in the oval, and descriptions of Buffalo that include Crystal Beach (right).

C&B Line

BUFFALO—QUEEN CITY OF THE LAKES

BUFFALO is the convenient gateway to the great summer resort sections of the Eastern United States and Canada. The tourist from the East, also, will find from Buffalo a delightful route by the C. & B. Line to Cleveland and Toledo, and to resorts of the utmost attractiveness at Cedar Point and Put-in-Bay.

Niagara Falls is only a short distance from Buffalo and transportation facilities are of the best. Upon arrival of C. & B. Line steamers at their dock in Buffalo, trolley cars are in readiness to take passengers direct to the brink of the cataract, while the service is frequent throughout the day on both the trolley and steam railroad lines.

Among the other resorts at Buffalo is Crystal Beach, a most delightful recreation ground. It is on the Canadian shore of Lake Erie and the trip by steamer from Buffalo is a joy in itself.

Buffalo is a city of beautiful homes, and Delaware Avenue is one of the famous residence thoroughfares of the United States. The old Milburn home, where President McKinley died and the Wilcox home, where President Roosevelt took the oath of office, are on this street.

Buffalo has a famous park, Delaware Park, in which is the Albright Art Gallery. Nearby is the building of the Buffalo Historical Society on the shore overlooking Gala Water.

The western part of New York State and many places of interest, in addition to Niagara Falls, may be visited by automobile tourists who take advantage of the special C. & B. Line automobile tourist service described on page 32.

Railroad tickets from eastern points to points of Cleveland will be accepted for passage on the C. & B. Line steamers between Buffalo and Cleveland described on page 26.

(For list of Buff...

BUFFALO
McKinley Monument   Albright Art Gal...
                         Delaware
Historical Building   Beautiful Dela...

Crystal Beach

Author's collection.

Through their experience operating a number of large and luxurious long distance steamers on the Great Lakes through the C & B Line, the LEEC officers knew exactly what the Crystal Beach Line needed. They and other investors in the company had considerably deeper pockets than the CBSFC, and commissioned the construction of two grand steamers, the Americana and her slightly younger, and better known twin, the Canadiana.

After the LEEC received their two vessels, the C & B Line included Crystal Beach in its marketing literature.

Eventually, the Buffalo and Crystal Beach Corporation purchased the assets of the Lake Erie Excursion Company. Under the leadership of George Hall Sr., the Buffalo and Crystal Beach Corporation started major expansion and modernization programs during the 1920s that transformed the park physically to the Crystal Beach Park most people today would recognize. They continued to operate the two steamers until the opening of the Peace Bridge precipitated declining steamer patronage and forced the sale of one of them.

The Great Depression forced Crystal Beach into

Author's collection.

Construction of the Peace Bridge precipitated declining patronage of the Lake Erie and Niagara River boat and ferry crossings and their eventual demise. The Crystal Beach Line was the last to succumb.

bankruptcy. However, the park and its one remaining steamer continued to operate. One of three companies that emerged from the bankruptcy and reorganization was the Crystal Beach Transit Company, which operated the Canadiana through 1956. Afterward, the Crystal Beach Line ceased.

After a dismal 1982 season, Crystal Beach Park fell into bankruptcy. Ramsi Tick (see image page in the Appendix), a Buffalo businessman, operated and managed the park for the receivers during 1983. Tick wanted to capitalize on nostalgia trends and recapture the golden years of Crystal Beach Park by

reintroducing boat service to Crystal Beach. Tick brought it back, but on a very limited basis. Emerging from bankruptcy, new owners were able to continue boat service for a few years, offering lake cruises to the park one to two days per week. Attempts to recapture the past continued with the reintroduction of music and dancing after thousands of dollars were spent refurbishing the park's commodious dance hall. Ramsi Tick, though no longer affiliated with the park, felt confident enough about the park's future that he purchased a decommissioned Block Island ferry and brought it to Buffalo to resume daily lake crossings to Crystal Beach.

Tick's operation experienced a number of operational setbacks, and more unfortunate is the fact that the ferry had little time to gain any momentum when it lost its only port of call when Crystal Beach Park closed forever after the 1989 season. Lake crossings to Crystal Beach ended forever.

From the passenger's perspective, the journey to Crystal Beach was an amusement unto itself. The steamers provided a two-hour boat ride - an hour to the

Author's collection.

Left: Heavy traffic entering Canada after crossing the Peace Bridge. A few years earlier these autos would have required a ferry, or their passengers would have sailed across by the Canadiana or some other vessel.

Above: The ferry Orleans was the last to operate the Niagara River crossing, ending service on May 15, 1951. Its operator, Clarance E. Fix said that costs and declining patronage forced taking the ferry out of service.*

park and an hour return. Evening cruises often featured music and dancing. A facet of the Crystal Beach Line that perhaps many of its patrons never recognized is the fact that the Line was a mass transit system that was subject to the same operational difficulties that a "public" mass transit system experienced - escalating operating expenses, maintenance issues, labor/personnel difficulties, aging equipment, and the one issue that amplified the others - declining patronage.

Most years, the operation of the steamers was uneventful, but like other mass transit systems, the Crystal Beach Line occasionally made headlines.

*"Bowing Out" Photo Caption. Buffalo Evening News, May 15, 1951.

The Early Steamers
CHAPTER 2

The Crystal Beach Line had five owners: John E. Rebstock, the Crystal Beach Steamboat and Ferry Company, the Lake Erie Excursion Company, the Buffalo and Crystal Beach Corporation, and the Crystal Beach Transit Company.

John Rebstock, founder of Crystal Beach, operated the Line until he formed the Crystal Beach Steamboat & Ferry Company late in 1891. Traditional history depicts Rebstock as the ticket agent, park manager, and sometimes captain of the steamers. He may have worn multiple hats during the early years of the park, but it is unlikely he piloted any of the Crystal Beach vessels. Steamship officers required licensing and there is no indication that Rebstock had any maritime training or spent any part of his life working on a Great Lakes steamer of any kind. His background as a hardware and stove dealer and a real estate developer indicate that he was a land lubber, and therefore spent his time on terra firma.

The Crystal Beach Steamboat and Ferry Company was a registered corporation with stock issued to its investors. John Rebstock was not one of the company's officers, though he was one of its directors.

The Lake Erie Excursion Company (LEEC) was

Author's collection.

organized according to a Certificate of Incorporation filed with the State of New York on May 24, 1899. A.T. Zillmer, an investor in the LEEC implies that that was when the LEEC became involved with Crystal Beach. Confirmation of LEEC's early involvement with Crystal Beach is evident when it leased the operations of the park and the Line in 1901 - years before the company took full control of the operation. The nature of their involvement before 1901 is unknown.

Crystal Beach opened on July 16, 1890, and so began the flotilla of steamers sailing there.

Twenty-five steamers comprised the Crystal Beach Line. Of these, three returned to the line after their original commission with a name change. Name changes were common. Following the sale of a vessel, the new owners often changed the ship's name. A name change was also a disguise to disassociate a rebuilt vessel with an earlier tragedy, like a fire, that brought about the rebuild. The rebuilt-and-renamed steamers could be considered a unique vessel, however, the unique "Official Number" assigned to each boat tracks its history essentially by

Right: Docked at the Crystal Beach pier is the steamer State of New York, which dates the photo to 1893 or 1895. The next time the State of New York sailed to Crystal Beach was 1906, and by that time, this original dock had been replaced.

Previous page: Another The canopied benches were originally on the grounds of Buffalo's Pan American Exposition of 1901. Crystal Beach purchased them afterward and placed them on the grounds in 1902. Based on that fact, and the steamers operating during 1902, the steamer docked at the pier most closely resembles the Darius Cole.

Author's collection.

Courtesy of Harvey Holzworth.

Courtesy of Cathey Herbert.

the hull from construction to destruction regardless of rebuild and/or name change. (Often, and for financial reasons, owners stripped their steamers down to their hulls and redeployed them as barges. This dramatic change of function would not affect a change to the assigned Official Number.) The steamers of the Crystal Beach Line are counted by their unique Official Number.

There are records of four other steamers having sailed to Crystal Beach, but their direct affiliations with the Line, if any, remains unknown. These steamers cannot be considered part of the Crystal Beach Line fleet, however, they did have a role in the nautical history of Crystal Beach, and therefore are duly represented.

Above: Crystal Beach Steamers Pearl and Gazelle docked on opposite of sides of the Crystal Beach pier, from the Harvey Holzworth collection.

Left: An earlier image of the Pearl and the Gazelle and the Crystal Beach pier from 1894. The Gazelle is docked, from the Cathy Herbert collection.

Officers

Crystal Beach Steamboat & Ferry Company

Courtesy of George Rebstock Jr.

John Evangalist Rebstock
Founder of Crystal Beach and Director of the
Crystal Beach Steamboat & Ferry Company.

Arthur W. Hickman, Esq.
President

Oliver O. Jenkins
Treasurer

Erastus C. Knight
Secretary

William Palmer, Esq.
Trustee
(then treasurer after Jenkins)

Author's collection.

Crystal Beach Steamboat and Ferry Company Mortgage Bond.

Crystal Beach Steamboat and Ferry Company Stock Certificate.

Courtesy of the Fort Erie Historical Museum, Ridgeway, Ontario.

Dove

The first steamer to sail to Crystal Beach was the *Dove*. Built by Alvin A. Turner in Trenton, Michigan, the *Dove* began sailing the Great Lakes in 1867. Buffalonians were not unfamiliar with the *Dove* - she worked the Niagara River transporting excursionists from Buffalo to Sour Spring Grove on Grand Island in 1889 and possibly earlier.

When John E. Rebstock leased the *Dove*, he did not have a name for his resort - at least not officially. That announcement came during the maiden voyage of the *Dove* to the resort, which was not on its opening day.

Rebstock hosted an inspection tour a few days before the official opening. Invited guests - an ambiguous description for a group of people to "inspect" the new resort, boarded the *Dove* on July 12, 1890. The guests included at least one news reporter and probably potential investors and others interested in establishing concessions at the resort. Perhaps on board were Erastus C. Knight (who would become mayor of Buffalo in the 1900s), Arthur W. Hickman (a prominent Buffalo attorney), and Oliver Jenkins (sheriff of Erie

County). These three men were to have important roles in the Crystal Beach Steamboat and Ferry Company.

Inspection of the resort was limited to what could be seen from the decks of the *Dove* because of *"...an unfortunate accident to the crib that was to form the outer extremity of the dock made a landing impossible."*

Before the *Dove* returned from the inspection voyage, its passengers had time to absorb the beauty

The first ad for Crystal Beach appeared in the Buffalo Courier on July 16, 1890.

Courtesy of the Milwaukee Public Library, Great Lakes Marine Collection.

The steamer Dove, quite possibly photographed at the pier belonging to Sour Spring Grove on Grand Island.

Courtesy of Cathy Herbert.

Courtesy of the Milwaukee Public Library, Great Lakes Marine Collection.

Top: Stearmer Dove at docked at Crystal Beach in 1890.
Above: The sidewheel steamer Dove, location unknown.

of the waterfront. Undoubtedly, drawing from his sales experience as a hardware dealer, Rebstock redirected the attention of his guests away from the dock and to the sweeping white sand beach while providing a captivating description of the grove that lay beyond the sand dunes. He would have described the pavilions and places of shelter that *"...will be constructed at once..."* and on the beach, *"...two large toboggans for bathers."*

One review described the new resort as *"wild and romantic...the shoreline of beautiful, unbroken sand made one fairly ache to get off his shoes and socks and run. In a few days, another trip would be made when it is hoped that another landing could be effected that those interested can inspect the Promised Land."*

Undeniably named after *"the shimmer of the setting sun reflecting off the sand,"* the resort was officially

announced during that inspection cruise, *"Crystal Beach."*

After the close of a successful inaugural season, John Rebstock announced his plan for a complete rehabilitation of the aged steamer for 1891 and the *Dove* went back to her owner. On June 24, 1891 while docked in Bay City, Michigan, someone discovered a fire in her hold that caused $3,000 in damage. Investigators suspected the fire began in a pile of oily rags. The fire could ultimately be the reason why the *Dove* never returned to Crystal Beach.

A month after the fire, her owner indicated that he had not made a decision whether to repair the steamer. For the next eight years, she remained charred and idle, and during this period, a tug presumably towed her to Toledo. There, in early June 1899, dynamite blew her hull to splinters.

The *Dove* almost met her demise less than two years after she was launched. On May 31, 1869 the propeller of the *Mayflower* struck the Dove's port bow so severely that she began taking on water at an alarming rate. In order to keep the Dove from sinking in deep water of the St. Clair River, her master beached her on the Canadian bank. The *Dove's* owners were later awarded over $14,000 dollars.

An ad for a trip on the Dove to Sour Spring Grove on Grand Island, N.Y. Buffalo Courier, July 1, 1889.

Pearl *Crystal*

Before the *Pearl's* long commission on the Crystal Beach Line, she ferried people between Detroit and other cities on the western shores of Lake Erie, and the leisure islands near Cedar Point.

Built in 1875 in Detroit by John P. Clark, the *Pearl* began her commission on the Crystal Beach Line in June 1891. She was the first steamer that the Crystal Beach Steamboat and Ferry Company (CBSFC) purchased. With a capacity of 1,300, the *Pearl* frequently could not accommodate all the people waiting on the Main Street dock that *"longed to romp on the fine sand beach."*

John Rebstock, near the close of Crystal Beach's successful debut season, made his intentions known to operate two steamers in 1891. The *Pearl*, however, operated solo - a two-steamer operation would begin in 1892. The daily crossings of the *Pearl* were uneventful until late in the summer of 1893, when the vessel began to appear in the headlines of the local papers.

The CBSFC sponsored the Buffalo Yacht Club's annual regatta on August 12, 1893 at Point Abino Bay. That afternoon, the *Pearl* departed for Crystal Beach with approximately 600 people on board. The weather was sunny and warm with a steady breeze and a fine chop on the water that made the reflection of the sun dance on its surface.

From the wheelhouse, Captain McLarty could see the Crystal Beach pier roughly three-quarters of a mile ahead. He gave the order to the crew to prepare for docking.

While lowering the ship fenders - bumpers that cushioned the hull against the dock - Fred Roberts lost his footing and tumbled overboard. Treading water in the wake from the paddle wheels, he waited for the *Pearl* to come about and rescue him. Hundreds on board watched Roberts as the steamer put distance between them.

The Pearl leaving Buffalo harbor on another run to Crystal Beach. Just below and to the right of the pilot house hangs a banner that reads this steamer for Crystal Beach.

Nobody threw Roberts a life jacket, life preserver, or one of the numerous wood chairs on deck to help him stay afloat. Apparently, there were no shouts of *"Man overboard!"* because the *Pearl* continued on her way for five minutes before Captain McLarty turned the steamer about. In those few minutes, Roberts disappeared.

During the subsequent investigation into the first fatality associated with Crystal Beach, some passengers stated that the crew was unresponsive to pleas to turn the ship about. When questioned about their own idleness for not throwing Roberts a life preserver immediately after they saw him plunge into the water, some insisted that Roberts began swimming to shore and therefore did not need one. Investigators also examined the spot where Roberts was standing at the moment he went overboard.

Conclusions of the investigation criticized the passengers for their unresponsiveness but it found the CBSFC liable for Roberts' death, noting that the rotten wood that supported Roberts broke under his weight. The CBSFC strongly objected claiming that the wood was decorative and not intended to support the weight of an individual. Additionally, according to Captain McLarty, it was against ship's regulations for anyone to hang off the side of the ship unprotected.

The Buffalo News later reported that an error had been made in the initial reports of this incident and that the deck hand that had fallen from the *Pearl* and drowned was J. H. Jones of Richford, New York. His body washed up on shore near the Crystal Beach pier a few days later.

Six years earlier, the *Pearl* came to the rescue of four survivors of the P. H. Walter after she sank during a sudden and severe storm on June 20, 1887. The *Pearl* and her crew rescued the tug's captain, his two sons, and the first mate in the early morning hours of June 21. Eight others on board, including the captain's wife, daughter, and a third son drowned.

The tug P. H. Walter along side sunken debris.

Pen and ink drawings of the Pearl and the Idle Hour from the Buffalo Courier Record, May 23, 1897.

The Pearl and Idle Hour became mixed up Saturday [June 12, 1894] in trying to make their docks and the latter jammed into the Pearl, crushing in her stem and compelling her to go into dry dock for repairs. The Pearl will be out again tomorrow.

- Buffalo Enquirer, June 13, 1892

"The Dove*, mentioned previously, was replaced in 1891 by another sidewheeler named* Pearl*. This craft served for a number of years, until one Independence Day it was caught at the dock in a storm and swung sideways on the beach. None of the 900 people aboard were injured..."*

- George J. Rebstock

George J. Rebstock, son of John Rebstock, was not the first person to tell this story; all of the accounts vary only slightly, if at all. All of them are incredibly understated in comparison to the period press coverage that found its way into the New York Times.

There where stiff breezes across Lake Erie, the kind of breezes that freshen the hot stale summer air with the scent of the lake waters. It was Saturday, July 7, 1900 and Crystal Beach was a sea of humanity; filled with people escaping the sweltering city.

Late that evening, the *Pearl* and another Crystal Beach steamer, the *Puritan* were tied to the Crystal Beach pier. At 10:00 PM, passengers began boarding the *Pearl*.

Flashes of lightning and the rumbling thunder from an approaching storm must have been somewhat disconcerting to those boarding, conjuring images of Great Lakes ship disasters of the recent past. With 900 people on board, the Pearl began backing away from the pier at 10:15 PM.

The severe gusts and driven rain struck the *Pearl* broadside. Although her boilers were hot and her engines were running, the craft did not have sufficient steam and forward momentum to overcome the storm's onslaught. The gales and driven waves started to push the steamer toward the beach.

The crew managed to aim the *Pearl's* prow in the direction of open water but the spinning paddle wheels only slowed her drift beachward.

A powerful jolt knocked passengers to the decks when the *Pearl's* stern hit bottom. Mired in sand, the stern acted like a pivot that allowed the waves and wind gusts to turn the *Pearl's* bow toward the dock. Each wave surge lifted the *Pearl* slightly off the bottom and as she floated briefly, the wind moved her closer to shore, then hit bottom again as the swell passed, sending a shudder throughout her frame. In very little time, the steamer was in eight feet of water, approximately 400 feet from the beach with her bow 15 feet from the pier.

As the storm raged, the *Puritan* attempted to wrench the *Pearl* off the bottom, but four attempts yielded four snapped towlines. The *Pearl* developed a severe port side list. Passengers started to panic because they could not stand upright and feared the steamer would be battered to pieces or capsize. It was time to evacuate the passengers.

A makeshift, 3-foot wide gangway extended from the pier to the bow of the *Pearl* and the evacuation of

Behind an unidentified tug, the Pearl is docked at the foot of Main Street.

passengers from her lower deck began. To assist the passengers, two crewmen handed off one passenger at a time to a deckhand on the gangway who handed that passenger to someone on the pier. Others tried to steady the gangway that rocked precariously with the *Pearl's* motion. Nearly an hour had passed from the time the *Pearl* left the dock and the evacuation of the first passenger.

There were 350 people still on board the *Pearl* at 12:15 AM. The last passenger stepped onto the pier at 1:10 AM. Tugs from Buffalo wrenched the beleaguered steamer from the lake bottom at 3:00 AM.

Afloat and with no apparent damage, the *Pearl* reached the Main Street dock at 5:30 AM, six hours late. Evidence of the ferocity of the storm was apparent there - it destroyed the Crystal Beach ticket office.

This was not the first time the *Pearl* had run aground. Long before her Crystal Beach Line commission, the *Pearl* worked the west end of Lake Erie. During a severe storm on September 13, 1878, a barge broke loose, pressed against the *Pearl* and snapped her from her moorings at Fairport, Ohio. She drifted about the lake and a few hours later ran aground roughly 660 feet away from her dock. Three days later, she was still aground in 3 feet of water, flooded and damaged. She remained beached for two more days before crews and tugs managed to refloat her.

Buffalo's inner harbor was usually hazy with smoke belched from the stacks of harbor tugs, lake freighters, and the industries that lined the inner harbor shores, such as it was on July 14, 1900. It is no wonder then that none of the 500 passengers on board the *Pearl* for a 2:00 PM departure to the Beach noticed wisps of smoke clinging to her decks from a fire burning in a coal bunker between her boiler and the port-side hull.

When it was discovered, the crew calmly asked the passengers to evacuate the vessel. To avoid panic, they told the passengers

The Pearl tucked up against the Main Street dock.

that mechanical problems prevented their departure. Shortly after, fire fighters arrived and stretched lines down to the bunker and extinguished the fire allegedly started by a fallen oil lamp.

All except a few passengers reboarded, and the *Pearl* set out for Crystal Beach. She had put considerable distance behind her, and as she sailed, the fire reignited.

The passengers were oblivious to the activity of the crew below decks who engaged the pumps and

continuously sprayed lake water onto the fire until the *Pearl* docked at the Crystal Beach pier.

A more thorough inspection of the coal bunkers revealed the fire, this time, had indeed been extinguished.

Fires on Great Lakes passenger and cargo steamers were common and always deadly. The list of the vessels lost to fire is lengthy. The Pearl and her passengers and crew were indeed lucky.

The Crystal Beach Steamboat and Ferry Company wintered the *Pearl* at Erie Basin where the basin's breakwall protected her and other vessels from winter storms and crushing lake ice. However, the breakwall did not afford the *Pearl* enough protection during a severe winter storm on November 12, 1900. The hull of the *Pearl*, weakened from the grounding, a fire, and age, split open from the rough water in the basin churned by the storm. Water flooded into the ship below decks and the 25-year old steamer sank in shallow water.

Rehabilitation work on the *Pearl* took place at the Union Dry Dock Company, then she returned to her commission on the Line in mid June as the *Crystal*.

Opening day, May 30, 1902, the *Crystal* operated solo on one of the busiest days of the year. It was one of those instances when the CBSFC found itself critically short of steamers. The *Crystal* probably carried more than her permitted capacity on each departure; however, many people were left behind at the Main Street dock and probably opted for a different resort.

Shuttered for winter in the Erie Basin is the Pearl (center) and another Crystal Beach Line steamer, the Gazelle (left). Photo from the Milwaukee Public Library, Great Lakes Marine Collection.

"The passenger stm. PEARL of the Crystal Beach Line will get out of drydock today after having received most extensive repairs. New arches have been put in and she has been refitted and repaired throughout. Capt. F.L.R. Pope, U.S. Inspector of Hulls, examined her officially yesterday and expressed himself as pleased with the soundness of the boat."

- Buffalo Evening Times, May 29, 1901

An ad for Crystal Beach with the departure schedules for the steamers Crystal and Puritan. Digitally enhanced for visual clarity. Buffalo Express, June 26, 1901.

Around 5:00 PM as she approached the Crystal Beach pier, she ran aground on a sand bar. She may have been able to free herself, but she was low in the water from too many people on board. She did not budge. Many passengers had no choice but to stand. A tug eventually pulled her free. Bottoming in sand, the Crystal was not damaged and after discharging her weary passengers, returned immediately to Buffalo. It was 9:00 PM when she reached the Main Street dock where hundreds still waited for passage to Crystal Beach.

The *Crystal* worked overtime, making many return runs past the last departing time on the schedule to bring everyone home.

Incidents involving the *Crystal* continued. On approach to the Main Street dock on July 7 at 5:30 PM, a log floating in the river became jammed between her portside paddle and hull and brought her engines to a sudden stop. She drifted to the dock at Washington Street, where her passengers disembarked. Men hacked and sawed at the obstruction for over three hours and finally removed it at 9:00 P.M. allowing the *Crystal* to return to service.

On August 31, 1902, during her 6:00 PM run to the resort, the *Crystal* experienced a structural failure that would take her off the Crystal Beach Line permanently. Steel rods anchored to the gallows frame that support a heavy iron walkway fractured and allowed the walkway to fall (presumably on top of the machinery). The *Crystal* came about and with approximately 300 on-board returned to Buffalo.

During mid-spring of 1903, announcements began appearing in the press about Crystal Beach's imminent season opening. The announced steamer line-up did not include the *Crystal*. Taken off the Line she would *"probably leave this port [Buffalo] as it is understood the vessel has been sold."*

There was no sale.

The reasons why the CBSFC stopped operating the *Crystal* are not clear, but the apparent structural failure that occurred that late August day of 1902 went unrepaired. Rather than spend additional money, John Rebstock put her up for sale, but if there were any purchase offers, a sale was never consummated. The CBSFC abandoned her near the ferry-crossing terminal at Ferry Street on Squaw Island.

There were high water conditions in the Niagara River during 1904, that by October, returned to

Opposite page: The Crystal awash in the Niagara River near the ferry landings on Squaw Island.

normal. As the high water subsided, the *Crystal's* hull settled on some pylons. The water level continued to drop, the *Crystal* tipped on her starboard side, and water poured in. During early spring of 1905, massive ice flows severely damaged her paddle box. Later, winter ice built up around her hull that often blocked the ferry landing. The *Crystal* became a menace to navigation, and owners of the ferries and the ferry landing were calling upon John Rebstock to remove the stricken steamer. In May of 1905,

Rebstock claimed that he had asked for bids to raise her. Having been stripped of anything of value, the *Crystal*, with obsolete engines, was considered by many on the lake and river not worth raising, noting the only thing of value in her was the ship's boiler.

The *Crystal* did not budge until December of 1905 when the sandsucker *Sandy Hook* wrenched her from her resting place. Taken to Erie Basin, where she sank as the *Pearl*, her machinery was removed and sold, and her remains dismantled.

The Crystal with a severe starboard list. Squaw Island in the background.

Below: The Crystal, abandoned but still afloat.

Above: The Crystal deep in water, listing to starboard, and her stack listing moreso.

Gazelle *Eagle*

Built in 1873, there is conflicting information about her builder, which could have been John P. Clark or George Irwin for John P. Clark. In either case, when the CBSFC purchased her for operation on the Crystal Beach Line, she was nearly 20 years old. She was the second of two steamers the company would own, and began her Crystal Beach commission in 1892.

The *Gazelle* would become a familiar steamer of the Line, with longevity near that of the Pearl, but with a less tumultuous history.

The first time the *Gazelle* made the press was July 16, 1897 when she collided with the steamer *Conestoga* while they both tried to negotiate past each other through a narrow slip. Neither vessel incurred any damage. Later that year, the *Gazelle* was involved in a more serious collision.

Indicative of Buffalo's prominence as a Great Lakes port at the time, the U.S. Government was busy constructing a breakwall to expand the outer harbor. The engineer on the job was Augustus Dilliot who leased the yacht *Glance* as his floating office. On Tuesday, September 28, 1897, the owner of the *Glance*, Captain George Moon of Black Rock, piloted the yacht toward the entrance to the inner harbor. On board with Captain Moon, were Dilliot and two others.

At left the Gazelle departs Buffalo. Note the antlers on the roof peak of the pilot house. Behind the Gazelle is the W. H. Rounds, built in Tonawanda New York by Parons & Humble in 1875. Right: The Gazelle heading for the open waters of Lake Erie.

Left: The Gazelle buttoned up for winter at Marquette, Michigan, circa 1880. Above: The tug C. F. Coughlin came into existence in 1895 as the Frank L. Bapst, and later modified from a side wheeler to a propeller. Allegedly her draft washed the Glance into the Gazelle's path.

Courtesy of the Milwaukee Public Library, Great Lakes Marine Collection

A tug, the *Frank L. Bapst* was as also heading for the inner harbor, towing a barge loaded with stone. Following the tug, and just off to her side was the *Gazelle*. The tug and the *Gazelle* were moving up river faster than the yacht. The *Glance* was first into the inner harbor, but the tug and the *Gazelle* were about to over take her. The tug passed the yacht, and the *Gazelle*, only seconds behind, was about to pass the yacht on its other side. According to Captain McCrea of the *Gazelle*, as the tug passed the yacht, the current generated from the tug's side wheel washed the yacht into the path of the *Gazelle*. The *Glance* received a glancing blow from the *Gazelle* that capsized and sank her. All four men on the Glance were thrown into the river, August Dilliot drowned.

At a later inquest, the survivors of the collision did not mention the tug but claimed simply that the *Gazelle* ran down the Glance.

The collision cost Captain McCrea his masters and first-class pilot's license, which put an end to his career. Based upon testimony, the *Gazelle* was moving too fast given the circumstances, and therefore McCrea was found in violation of Rule V1 of the Rules and Regulations for Pilots on the Great Lakes.*

The *Gazelle's* next press worthy event came on August 9, 1898. She departed the Main Street dock in Buffalo at 9:00 PM and cruised effortlessly past the harbor walls. Approximately half way to Crystal Beach, she developed unspecified mechanical problems and could no longer continue under her own power.

Adrift in the lake, the *Gazelle's* crew managed to signal the harbor tug *Grace Danforth* that towed the crippled steamer with her passengers to the Crystal Beach pier. Whether the tug towed the *Gazelle* back to Buffalo for repairs or if they were fashioned for her at Crystal Beach was not disclosed.

The *Gazelle* was involved with another collision on June 21, 1899 when the steamer *Lewiston* struck her bow, but only slightly. Damage to the *Gazelle* was merely cosmetic.

Left, the Lewiston collided with the Gazelle, albeit slightly in 1899.

Above, the steamer Conestoga, kissed the Gazelle as they tried to squeak past each other in a narrow channel.

* Rule V1, basically, forbids running a steamer at a greater speed than good judgment would permit.

The Glance - sunk by the Gazelle.

The Gazelle after a name change and her pilot house antlers replaced by an eagle.

It must have been a very low tide during the evening of August 24, 1900 when the shoe of the *Gazelle's* propeller struck a rock approximately 300 feet from the Crystal Beach pier at the start of her 9:00 PM departure.

She drifted for an hour until the tug *Glenora* arrived and nosed her back to the pier. The *Gazelle's* passengers transferred to the *Puritan* for passage back to Buffalo.

The CBSFC may have opted to sell the *Gazelle* to underwrite the restoration of the *Pearl* after her sinking. The *Pearl* was a larger vessel with a higher capacity than the *Gazelle*. If capacity was their only basis for their decision, they may have regretted it since the *Pearl*, as the *Crystal*, did not last long.

Daniel Mahoney of Buffalo purchased the *Gazelle* and renamed the steamer *Eagle*. The *Eagle* sailed to Crystal Beach when demand necessitated, but never returned to the Crystal Beach Line after 1901.

Mahoney then sold it to George P. Gubbins of Chicago. Records dated December, 27, 1908 list the Eagle as abandoned by the underwriters and burned off Chicago Harbor by order of the U.S. Government.

Auction *of the* Pearl *&* Gazelle

After five seasons, the CBSFC began operating steamers to Crystal Beach on Sunday. There are two factors that could have brought about this change in operating policy. John Rebstock opened the Crystal Beach International Assembly in 1895 (which ceased operations after the summer of 1896) and the anticipated patronage of Assembly's programs may have necessitated steamer operation on Sunday. If not for this reason, then perhaps initiating Sunday operations was borne out of necessity to generate as much income as possible. The CBSFC was having trouble paying its debts, so rather than leaving the steamers idle at the dock on the busiest excursion day of the week, Crystal Beach and the steamers were put into operation on Sundays.

Evidence of the CBSFC's financial liabilities appeared in the press on February 25, 1895 when the Deputy Clerk of the United States Court, D. C. Forlong, issued a warrant authorizing the public auctions of the *Pearl* and *Gazelle*. Coal dealer H. K. Wicks initiated the proceedings against the CBSFC to recover over $36,000 owed for several tons of coal furnished to both steamers during 1894 that the CBSFC never paid for. There were seven other actions for judgment for various amounts filed against each of the boats. The projected income from the auction of the steamers was between $25,000 and $35,000, which was insufficient to meet *all* the encumbrances. Because the steamers were not bonded, Judge Coxe of the United States District Court ruled in favor of the coal dealer to force the auction to gain payment.

Deputy United States Marshal J. V. Kane decided to hold the auction on March 6, 1895 at 10:00 AM.

The morning of the auction, a large crowd of marine men assembled at the auction site to bid on the boats. Meanwhile, the CBSFC and H. K. Wicks & Co. had agreed to settle. When Marshal Kane arrived, J. H. Rebstock [Joseph H. Rebstock was John's younger brother], asked that the auction be postponed until 1:00 PM to give the company time to arrange a settlement.

Both companies came to terms and the legal action was formally suspended. The terms of the settlement were not disclosed nor were the settlements of the other encumbrances.

Puritan

In 1893 the Crystal Beach Steamboat and Ferry Company leased the *Puritan* to operate regularly with the company's two owned vessels. She was brought in again to work the line in 1897, 1898 and 1901.

The *Puritan's* 1901 commission was abruptly halted during the early morning hours of July 14, 1901. Docked at the facilities of the Cleveland and Buffalo Transit Company, a night watchman discovered a fire below decks and amidship at about 4:00 AM. By the time the watchman was able to sound a fire alarm to wake the crew asleep in their quarters, the fire spread significantly, breaching the deck above.

Although the crew tried to extinguish the fire, it had grown too large for their efforts to make a difference. Forced to abandon ship, some deckhands managed to retrieve their personal belongings and escape the burning vessel. Others, trapped by the flames, were forced to jump overboard. By the time the fireboats arrived and began pumping water onto the fire, the *Puritan's* upper decks were completely engulfed.

From what little remained of the *Puritan* and the limited forensic capabilities of the time, inspectors could only determine that the fire began in or near the boiler room. Edward Gaskin, formerly an agent of the Buffalo Drydock Company, assessed the damage at $14,532.23

John Rebstock had to replace the *Puritan* immediately and negotiated a short-term lease for the steamer *Lincoln* from the International Line. The *Lincoln* was considerably smaller than the *Puritan*, and operated until the arrival of the *White Star* from Toronto – a steamer comparable to the *Puritan*.

Damage to the Puritan was not severe enough for her owners to scuttle her; however, she would never again transport excursionists dressed in their finest for a holiday at Crystal Beach or any other waterfront resort. After what little remained of her upper decks was stripped away, the Puritan was rebuilt as a tug, and re-christened the *Sandy Hook* and shuttled between Buffalo and Ashtabula, Ohio towing scows behind her.

A very busy Main Street dock in and out of the water. The Puritan holds a prime dock position. Note the six different steamer ticket offices. The Crystal Beach ticket office is third from the left.

Previous page: The Puritan departs Buffalo for Crystal Beach. A close inspection of the photo reveals the destination on her stack. Above: Impossible to see in small scale, the banner hanging off the railing toward the rear of the second deck indicates the Puritan is on her way to Eldorado Beach on Grand Island.

"Buffalo, June 24. - The steamer Kearsarge came in with a broken wheel today and did not take a tug. In passing the excursion steamer Puritan she took a sheel [sic] and struck the Puritan aft, doing about $50 damage."

- Milwaukee Library Scrapbook
June 25, 1897

"The steamer Puritan went down to Tonawanda late on Monday night. Early yesterday morning she took on a large excursion party for Crystal Beach. A wind made the ride rather rough, and quite a number of passengers were sick. The Puritan took the party back to Tonawanda last night."

- Buffalo Morning Express
June 29, 1898

"The excursion season opened with a rush yesterday. Early in the morning crowds were at the dock awaiting the sailing of the first boat for the beach resorts. The Crystal Beach boat had an unusually large crowd to handle. The large stm. Puritan was the only boat on the run and it is said she carried over 5,000 persons to the beach. The boat, notwithstanding the heavy traffic, got away on schedule time. The Niagara took a goodly number of excursionists to Woodlawn Beach during the day."

- Buffalo Morning Express
May 31, 1900

"In holding its popularity with strangers as well as with the Buffalo people, crowds are flocking to this popular resort. The bathing at Crystal is a great attraction. The stms. Crystal and Puritan are making 10 trips daily from the foot of Main St. and there are many attractions at the beach."

- Buffalo Daily Courier
July 13, 1901

Above: An ink drawing of the Puritan from the Buffalo Courier Record, May 23, 1897.

State of New York

John Rebstock anticipated that his Crystal Beach International Assembly (CBIA) would become immediately popular. He announced that the steamer *State of New York* would sail to Crystal Beach to accommodate the increased demand generated by the Assembly. Whether she actually sailed to Crystal Beach in 1895 is uncertain. Between 400 and 500 attended the opening ceremonies - not even a boatload for any of the CBSFC steamers. There is no evidence in the press that attendance at the CBIA did anything but decline, so additional steamers would be unwarranted.

The *State of New York's* first excursions to Crystal Beach came a few years before the Crystal Beach International Assembly materialized. On a particularly busy July 20, 1893, she made two trips to the park from Buffalo in addition to those made by the *Pearl* and the *Gazelle*.

Christened the *City of Mackinac* in 1883, the Detroit and Cleveland Steam Navigation Company (D & C

Line) built and operated her until they sold her to the C & B Line in 1892. Her new owners changed her name to the *State of New York*.

The C & B Line steamer served on the Crystal Beach Line for two entire seasons beginning in 1906.

Before her commission started, Rebstock went to Detroit to inspect the work outfitting her for operation on the Line. Originally, the steamer had plenty of staterooms to accommodate approximately 300 for overnight excursions. To increase her capacity for the short run between Buffalo and Crystal Beach, workers were dismantling all of the staterooms. After delivery of new furniture more appropriate for short, informal runs, she departed Detroit for Buffalo and her new commission.

A bit of scandal made the press about John J. Cassin, Captain of the *State of New York* (See Images page in the Appendix) and his estranged wife, Lulu.

People already on board and those boarding for the steamer's 2:00 PM departure could not have missed Lulu Cassin's verbal altercation with a deckhand who refused

Opposite page: Passengers on board the State of New York docked at the Crystal Beach pier.

STEAMER "STATE OF NEW YORK" ARRIVING
AT CRYSTAL BEACH

All post cards from the author's collection.

CHUTE SHOOTERS AND SURF BATHERS AT CRYSTAL BEACH

Hammond Press   THE NEW PIER AT CRYSTAL BEACH

The State of New York at Crystal Beach in post cards. Above: A rare post card of the State of New York approaching the Crystal Beach pier. Above right, the State of New York at Crystal Beach's first pier. Right, the State of New York at the second pier.

to let her board in spite of her valid ticket. Lulu had not seen her children in some time, and she suspected her husband had them on board with him. Rather than waste time arguing, she ran to the Franklin Street Police Station and swore out a warrant of nonsupport.

Lulu claimed she had sworn out a similar warrant months ago that the police never served. Officers at the station told her it would take a number of days before they could serve the new warrant. Lulu exploded with rage and language (which the Buffalo Courier noted was unsuitable to print), exclaiming that Cassin was close by and the warrant could be served immediately. To the satisfaction of the irascible Lulu, a policeman managed to reach the *State of New York* before she departed and arrested Cassin. Shortly afterward, an officer of the Crystal Beach Line posted bail for Cassin who then returned to his ship. The outcome of the Cassin's familial dispute was not published.

Eventually the *State of New York* became the property of the Columbia Yacht Club of Chicago that converted the vessel into a clubhouse in 1936.

A. J. Tymon

Launched at Port Dover in Canada during 1884, *William Alderson* was the first name given to this steamer. A fire damaged her seven years later, and after rebuilding the steamer at a Toronto yard, her owners renamed the vessel *A. J. Tymon.*

The *"Tymon"* was another steamer that worked the Crystal Beach Line during the exceptionally high demand periods during 1894. The *Tymon* also sailed between Buffalo and Port Colborne regularly during 1894 - individuals were notified to contact J. H. Rebstock, General Manager (John Rebstock's brother) for excursion rates.

During her relatively long life, the *Tymon* would receive two more name changes. Her final listing is under the ownership of the Corporation of the City of Toronto in 1928.

Seen here on the Hiawatha Route is the A. J. Tymon as the Ojibway - her third name.

Nellie

Nellie came into existence as a schooner in 1882 at Mount Clemens, Michigan, and reconfigured into a steamer four years later in Detroit.

She came to Buffalo from Port Huron, Ohio in 1894 for the Grand Island excursion trade. The only day the *Nellie* provided service to Crystal Beach was August 7, 1894 when members of the Canadian Liberal Party overran the park celebrating the success of a reform movement in a recent election. That day, the *Tymon* transported passengers between the Beach and Victoria, Ontario.

Apparently there was sufficient steamer service to Grand Island, and by October 1894, the *Nellie* was put up for auction in Tonawanda by her creditors. Frank J. Biasing became the owner of the *Nellie* on October 29, 1894 when he paid $2,000 for the steamer.

Eventually she made her way back to Detroit where she burned to the water line on May 18, 1903. She functioned as a sand barge during her remaining years and was finally reported as abandoned and out of commission in 1914.

Nellie at an unidentified location.

Garden City

Below, the Garden City departs Buffalo, the coal dock behind her. Following page: the Garden City docked at an unidentified location.

Garden City served on the Crystal Beach Line during the 1896 season. Not a regular steamer on the Niagara Frontier, the CBSFC leased the steamer from the Niagara, St. Catharines & Toronto Navigation Company of Toronto. The John Doty Engine Works built her in 1892.

Her entire operation on the line was uneventful except for the evening of August 19, 1896 when misinterpreted signals caused a collision with the steamer *Avon*. A steel hulled freighter, there was no damage to the *Avon*, but the stern of the *Garden City* incurred some damage. The excited passengers were without injury; however, their excitement rose to panic when *"some low-browed idiot"* screamed that the steamer was sinking.

Garden City remained an active steamer until scrapped sometime during the 1930s.

Shrewsbury

The *Shrewsbury* had three previous owners before she came to Buffalo in 1896 after the Sloan and Cowles Company purchased her. She originated in Bath, Maine in 1887, a product of the Bath Iron Works.

Ten years later, the *Shrewsbury* took the first picnic group of the season to Crystal Beach on May 15, 1897 - weeks before the regular steamers of the line were ready for operation. The *Shrewsbury* was not a regular steamer on the Line, though pressed into service when there was sufficient demand.

Later in 1897, the Thousand Islands Steamboat Company purchased her for service on the St. Lawrence River. In order for her to fit through the locks and canals, the William Murphy Company narrowed her hull by 44 inches. This change and other modifications cost $10,000. At the completion of these changes, her owners rechristened her *"New York."*

Bay Transportation Company purchased the *New York* for the western Lake Erie Islands trade in 1907. A year later, stripped of her engine for use in a different steamer, the tug *Logan* towed her to the Great Lakes Engineering Works in Ecorse, Michigan where she was dismantled.

Left: The Shrewsbury after her waist reduction in operation as the New York, most likely somewhere on the St. Lawrence. Following page: Superior, the "tub" of the Crystal Beach Line.

"Not a handsome boat" is the phrase used by the press to describe the *Superior* when she arrived in Buffalo. In short, *Superior* was a tub. She helped to fill the loss of the *Puritan* when her upper decks went up in flames in 1901. Prior to her Crystal Beach Line commission, she transported passengers between Cleveland, Ohio and Euclid Beach, another burgeoning amusement resort just east of Cleveland.

The Ohio park owned the *Superior* since 1897. After working the 1901 season on the Crystal Beach Line, she returned to Euclid Beach. By 1917, she was the property of the Pringle Barge Line that converted her into a tug and renamed her the *Walter R. Pringle*. It burned at the head of Stag Island in the St. Clair River on May 6, 1920. Beached on west side of the island, her remains were blown up during November, 1958.

Superior

America

John Rebstock had to scramble to replace the burned out *Puritan* in 1901. The steamer *White Star* would serve as her ultimate replacement but until her arrival, Rebstock took the International Navigation Company up on their offer to use their steamer *America* to fill in.

America first ran excursionists between Chicago and Michigan City during the first three years after her completion in 1898. Her only year on Lake Erie was 1901. Demand for her on the Niagara River was heavy on July 21, 1901, but she did manage to make one trip from Buffalo to Crystal Beach that day.

Late in 1901, Alfred Booth purchased the vessel to run between Duluth and the north shore ports of Lake Superior. Her life came to an untimely end on June 7, 1928 when she hit a reef off Isle Royale. It punctured her hull and she sank on the reef with only her bow and pilot house above water and a severe list to port.

An attempt to raise during 1929 failed and she ultimately slipped beneath the water - 85 feet at the bow, 4 feet at the stern.

Her shallow grave makes her a popular sight for divers, as well as tourists who can easily see the steamer from the surface.

Courtesy of the Milwaukee Public Library, Great Lakes Marine Collection.

Previous page: Built in Wyandotte, Michigan by the Detroit Dry Dock Company, America began sailing in 1898. At right, the America before slipping into a shallow grave off Isle Royale.

Lincoln Premier

Greyhound was the first name of the steamer built by Simpson-Melancthon in Hamilton, Ontario for Gooderman & Worts Brewing Company of Toronto. They owned and operated her from her completion in 1888 until 1899 when the brewer sold her to R.W. Hamlin of St. Catharines. Hamlin changed the steamer's name to *Lincoln*.

Lincoln was brought to Buffalo that year to shuttle passengers to Chippawa, Ontario on the Niagara River just upstream from the Horseshoe Falls. This route operated in conjunction with the Niagara River Railway that connected to the Great Gorge Route trolley through the Niagara River gorge. From the Great Gorge Route, a steamer for Toronto could be boarded in Lewiston, New York, or Queenston, Ontario.

During 1901, more steamers were operating between Buffalo and Niagara Falls than in previous years - all vying for a share of the increased tourist trade generated by the thousands that came from across North America to see Buffalo's Pan American Exposition. Many of these tourists took side trips to see the falls.

Preious page: Before she was the Lincoln, she was the Greyhound.

The competition between the steamers and rail service between Buffalo and the Falls was stiff, and perhaps the *Lincoln's* owner saw a greener horizon by leasing her to the Crystal Beach Line. Undoubtedly the lake and river resorts all benefited from the influx of tourists and Crystal Beach could have lost a significant amount of business without the *Lincoln*.

In March 1904, the *Lincoln* sank at her winter moorings in Detroit in 22 feet of water - with only her smokestack visible. In one month, she was afloat and repairs were underway.

Like the *Puritan*, everything above the *Lincoln's* hull line was destroyed by fire on April 7, 1905. Again she was rebuilt and renamed Premier and started the 1906 excursion season sailing to Pelee Island until she returned to the Crystal Beach Line early in August 1906 and operated for the balance of the season.

Her final full season commission on the Crystal Beach Line began on July 4, 1907.

Another fire spelled doom for the steamer on November 13, 1920 while docked at Bruce Mines, Ontario.

Arundell

The *Arundell* came from builder David Bell of Buffalo. He operated the steamer, providing excursions on the Niagara River upon her completion in 1878. Bell sold the steamer during the winter of 1880-81 and her new owner modified her extensively, including widening her decks by nearly six feet.

After $10,000 worth of improvements, the *Arundell* sailed between Bay City and Alpena, Michigan, and later, between Port Huron and Detroit, Michigan and the Lake Erie islands.

Arundell returned to Buffalo to work the Crystal Beach Line for the 1903 season. She worked the Thousand Islands routes in 1904, and returned for her last Crystal Beach Line commission in 1905.

Back on the Thousand Islands routes, she ran aground on a shoal late in June 1908. Slightly damaged, repairs were made to her at Kingston, Ontario.

On October 18, 1911 she caught fire at Douglas, Michigan, and burned to her hull and then used as a barge afterward. By 1919, the *Arundell* was registered in the New York City area. Two years later, presumably new owners renamed the barge *Brewster* and towed her to North Carolina. She sank after colliding with the freighter *Lake Stirling* on the James River on April 21, 1922.

Courtesy of Harvey Holzworth.

Right: The Arundell at an unidentified location. On the following page, she takes on passengers at Oswego, New York.

Idlewild

Above: Idlewild and behind her, the Darius Cole - another steamer of the Crystal Beach Line. Previous page: Idlewild with a boatload of excursionists.

Many steamers on the Great Lakes came from Wyandotte, Michigan. On May 3, 1879, the Detroit Dry Dock Company launched another, the *Grace McMillan*. Built for the Detroit Steam Navigation Company, she was renamed *Idlewild* in 1881.

The White Star Line of Detroit purchased *Idlewild* in 1899 and her first commission on the Crystal Beach Line was the 1903 season. The following year she worked between Buffalo and Idlewild Park on Grand Island and returned to the Crystal Beach Line in 1905.

Her history on the Line is uneventful except for a very windy August 15, 1905 when she lost her rudder on her way to the Beach. Driven by the wind and waves, she reportedly drifted for five hours before someone on shore at Windmill Point saw her in distress and summoned tugs. The reported time she spent adrift seems exaggerated. Having to keep to a schedule, its unlikely that officials from the Crystal Beach Line would not have noticed her absence long before five hours transpired. Tugs eventually towed her back to port.

The *Idlewild* worked the Crystal Beach Line again during 1907, but only on demand.

Registry indicates her dismantling in 1914. Her movement over the next five years is unknown, then in 1919, she appeared in the New York City area, registered as a barge. Her final record on March 3, 1923 shows her surrendered with hull lying at Peekskill, N.Y.

The Darius Cole in Buffalo while on the Crystal Beach Line, as noted on her wheel house.

Darius Cole

Launched at the Globe Iron Shipyard in July of 1895, the steamer *Darius Cole "Cole"* was not entirely new. Her engine came from the defunct steamer, *Dunlap*. Three months later, her owners announced that a new engine would be built for her because the used engine did not perform as expected.

The *Cole* came to Buffalo to work the Crystal Beach Line in 1902 - one of those years that the Line was having difficulty obtaining steamers. The Line started the season with only one steamer, the *Crystal*, which on opening day ran aground, bringing operations to a halt.

Arriving in early June, it took two weeks to prepare the *Cole* for service that included a cleaning from stem to stern and a fresh paint job. Her first trip to Crystal Beach came on the evening of June 18 - a special excursion that would leave the dock at 8:00 PM. The cruise featured music; passengers were treated to strawberries and ice cream.

Not all of the *Darius Cole's* excursions to Crystal Beach were as celebratory as her first.

An accident involving the *Darius Cole* on the night of August 20, 1903 marred what would have otherwise been a perfect excursion history on the Line. Captain Phillips was at the helm and ahead he could see the pier lights extending in a line out into the darkness of the lake seemingly suspended in mid air. It was approximately 8:30 PM as Phillips routinely took the *Cole* west approximately 1,000 feet past the pier then rounded back to make the approach and landing. Glare from the

Excursions

Society Moonlight
—
Crystal Beach
and Up the Lake

WEDNESDAY EVENING,
JUNE 18th

First trip of that Beautiful Steamer
DARIUS COLE

Band Concert on Boat. Round trip 25c.
Leave Main Street at 8 p. m.

From the Buffalo Express, June 17, 1902.

landing lights on the dock and their reflection off the water blinded Phillips to a small sailboat approximately 100 feet in front of the steamer and slightly to port. That sailboat was about to cross the *Cole's* path.

The four young people on the sailboat had to have seen the *Cole* approaching for some time, though they never made any course correction to avoid her. Perhaps they misjudged the speed of their own small craft and thought they could outrun her safely. Perhaps they were

trying to change their direction, but for reasons unknown, inexperience maybe, their efforts failed. As the steamer drew ever closer, the panic escalated compounding their struggles to avoid a collision.

The sailboat had no running lights for Captain Phillips to see. When he did see a silhouette of the sailboat, it was dead ahead with the *Cole* bearing down on her. Phillips immediately signaled the engine room, full speed astern.

The volume of the low pulsating bellow from the

The rescued young man was William Hunt from Ridgeway, also 20 years old who survived the collision without injury. The women sustained serious injuries. Seventeen-year-old Tilly Riedeman suffered a fracture to her right arm and two scalp wounds. Emma Ellis endured a broken left shoulder, scalp wounds, and a severe cut to her left ear that nearly severed it off. On board the *Cole,* the ship's purser tended to the women as the *Cole* returned to Buffalo. At the Main Street dock, an ambulance was waiting to take the women to Emergency Hospital. Leonard Schooley's body was never recovered.

steamer's engine and the paddles striking the water drowned out the screams of the passengers on the sail boat. In an instant, the *Cole's* bow struck the stern of the sailboat and ground it under. Phillips ordered the engines stopped so the paddles would not strike anyone.

Sailors lowered lifeboats, where in the water, they paddled in the direction of the cries for help in the darkness. They rescued two young women and one young man. A fourth passenger in the sailboat, twenty-year old Leonard Schooley from Ridgeway, Ontario drowned. Schooley was sitting in the stern of the sailboat directly in line with the *Darius Cole's* bow.

The *Cole* was involved in another minor collision two years later while berthed at the Main Street dock. Another lake steamer, the *Northwest* was positioning herself at the dock when her stern swung into the stern of the *Cole.* Some of the *Cole's* stanchions and deck rails were damaged.

The *Darius Cole's* Crystal Beach Line commission ended after the 1905 season. In 1906, her owners changed her name to *Huron* and in 1921 to the *Colonial.* After a fire and subsequent beaching in Barcelona, New York, she was towed to Dunkirk, New York and scrapped in 1925.

Wyandotte

Brought to Buffalo in 1904, the *Wyandotte's* two-year commission on the Crystal Beach Line was uneventful. The only thing remarkable about her entire history is that from the time of her construction in 1892 until her demise in 1940, she had eleven different owners, three of them in 1904 alone. During her existence, she also had three other names, *City of Fort Myers, Alatex,* and *Dolphin.*

The Detroit Dry Dock Company built *Wyandotte* for G. N. McMillen of Detroit. Her other owners included the Country of Panama during 1924 and 1925. Its last recorded owner is the G. M. Cox Shipyard of New Orleans, and she is recorded as abandoned in 1941.

Wyandotte, 1925 or earlier. Starting in 1926 she was the City of Fort Myers.

Fort Erie Grove, which would evolve to become Erie Beach, enjoyed considerable business before Crystal Beach began eroding its customer base in 1890. Business had been so good, the people often had to wait for two or three departures before their turn in line to board a "Grove" steamer. Fortunately, the Grove was just across the lake from Buffalo and the time to wait was short.

During 1887, three years before Crystal Beach opened, the steamer *Mascotte* came to Buffalo specifically for the Fort Erie Grove trade, and she began her commission in August. It was the first time she had been on the Niagara Frontier.

Detroit interests purchased the steamer in 1895, and she did not return to the Niagara Frontier until leased by the Crystal Beach Line for the 1904 season. It was the only year she worked the Line.

Mascotte partially burned in winter quarters, January 28, 1934 in the Chicago River. The U.S. Corps of Engineers advertised for bids to remove the wreck in June 1948.

Mascotte

Above, Flora with her route from Cleveland to Port Stanley, Ontario emblazoned on her paddle wheel housing.

Urania

Another single season steamer of the Crystal Beach Line was Urania. When she began her 1904 commission on the line, she was nearly thirty years old. Built in 1875 by Wolf & Davidson of Milwaukee for the Northwestern Transportation Company, her original name was Flora. In 1899, William Woolatt of Wakerville, Ontario became her owner and changed her name to Urania. Her primary route ran between Port Stanley, Ontario and Cleveland.

Her 1904 season on the Crystal Beach Line was uneventful.

Woolatt sold her in 1905 to the Erie Transportation Company. This new company changed her name back to Flora with the intention of running her between Buffalo and Erie, Pennsylvania. They originally announced they would change the name of the steamer to *Keystone* but that name change never occurred.

While in Chicago, the Flora burned late in 1912 just before going up for sale by the sheriff to pay creditors. There were three men on board, one lost his life. The steamer was a total loss.

Urania as the Flora with a less attractive paint job.

White Star

The White Star discharging passengers at an undisclosed port. Her early years were spent working the excursion trade of Montreal, Quebec. She also had ports on Lake Ontario, and sailed between Buffalo and Dunkirk, New York.

During 1901, a tremendous influx of tourists visiting Buffalo's Pan American Exposition meant increased business at other local attractions. Many of the out-of-towners made side trips to the source of the exposition's power, Niagara Falls. The White Star was one of the steamers working the water route between Buffalo and Niagara Falls that year and benefited from the draw of the exposition.

Five years later, the White Star was on the Crystal Beach Line. On June 3, 1906, while en route to Crystal Beach, a casting on one of her cylinders broke. Unable to proceed under her own power, the tugs Alpha and Cascade came to her assistance and towed the ailing steamer to the Crystal Beach pier. After her passengers disembarked, the tugs towed her back to Buffalo. Later that evening, both tugs towed the crippled White Star back to Crystal Beach to pick up people for a scheduled 7:30 departure. That return trip finally arrived in Buffalo at 11:00 PM. The White Star was out of commission for the next two days while a piston casing was fabricated and fitted.

W. C. White built the White Star in Montreal, Quebec. She had a very long life, but not all of it as a passenger steamer. She burned to her hull in Hamilton, Ontario in January 1926, then was used as a barge afterward. Twenty-two years later, the Simpson Sand Company of Brockville, Ontario transformed the White Star into a sand dredge. In 1976, she was reportedly became a breakwall at Brockville.

Argyle

PT. DOVER, O.

Courtesy of Walter Lewis, Maritime History of the Great Lakes

*B*uilt by William Jamieson in the yard of E. W. Rathbun & Company, she was christened *Empress of India* at her launching in 1876 at Mill Point (now Deseronto), Ontario. Immediately after her build-out, the *"Empress"* worked the Toronto Excursion trade. Her destinations included the Humber River, Oakville, Burlington Beach and Hamilton. While on an excursion in the Grand River in Galt, Ontario, mechanical difficulties developed that made the direction of the steamer uncontrollable and she was washed over a 12-foot tall milldam - eight passengers died.

After repairs, the *"Empress"* continued serving the Toronto excursion trade until 1883 when her owner saw greater profits in the Niagara region. For many years, she carried passengers across Lake Ontario to Port Dalhousie, through the first lock of the Welland Canal where she discharged her passengers.

After a lengthening in 1899, she was renamed Argyle, and came to Buffalo from Kingston, Ontario late in June of 1907 for a one-year commission on the Crystal Beach Line. Her only season on the Line was uneventful.

Her name was changed to *Grimsby*, and then to *Frontier*. In 1918 she sank while in Chatham, Ontario. Then her upper decks burned and her hull was raised and scrapped in 1920.

Previous page: A post card of the Argyle on a rainy day in Port Dover, Ontario. Above: As the Empress of India.

"...it seemed as if the rudder would not work, and when at last it did, it unfortunately was turned the wrong way, and the boat headed directly for the fall, and before those on board could realize their position the steamer drifted broadside to the fall, and in a moment went crashing over into the boiling water beneath."

- *"Sad Accident at Galt"*
Meaford Monitor,
Friday, May 31, 1878

Ossifrage

Steamer "Ossifrage," Chatham, Ont., Canada

Author's collection.

The CBSFC tried to lease the *Ossifrage* for the 1891 season but its owner had other plans for the steamer (see page 19). The *Ossifrage* eventually had a commission on the Crystal Beach Line, but it would not begin until 1908. By that time, the Crystal Beach Steamboat and Ferry Company passed into history, and the Lake Erie Excursion Company owned Crystal Beach Park and all associated assets.

Crystal Beach had become so popular that its newly launched steamer, the Americana with a capacity of 3,500,

Ossifrage at Knife Island, Lake Superior, 1888. Photograph by G. A. Newton, courtesy Northeast Minnesota Historical Center, Duluth, MN, S2381 b1f5

often left people at the Main Street dock after being fully loaded. In order to increase the capacity of the Line, the Lake Erie Excursion Company leased the *Ossifrage*, which stayed on the Crystal Beach Line for two years.

F. W. Wheeler and Company launched the *Ossifrage* during May of 1886 at Bay City, Michigan. Her entire history seems to be uneventful except for a number of rebuilds and a lengthening in 1892. Her end came accidentally while being towed in the Northumberland Strait in the Atlantic Ocean, where she struck a shoal and foundered in September 1919.

Ossifrage was the last steamer of the parade of steamers that comprised the Crystal Beach Line from 1890 through 1909. When the Lake Erie Excursion Company launched the Canadiana - a near duplicate of the Americana, the Line could boast a stable, wholly owned fleet of palatial steamers.

Others on the Run

CHAPTER 3

During the early years, five steamers sailed to Crystal Beach that were not vessels of Crystal Beach Line. The Cleveland and Buffalo Transit Company operated two of them. This discovery is not a blinding revelation given the fact that a number of people held executive positions on the C & B Line and the Lake Erie Excursion Company. Therefore, on occasion, a C & B Line steamer not leased to the Crystal Beach Line made an excursion to the park.

Understanding the nature of the visits by the other three steamers is not as easy. Crystal Beach Line steamers occasionally made a special excursions from Dunkirk, New York and Erie, Pennsylvania. Its possible that the Crystal Beach Line permitted other vessels from these longer distance ports to dock when their own vessels were unavailable due to local demand.

The extent to which Crystal Beach shared in the gross receipts of these special excursions is unknown, as is the frequency of the privileged docking. Evidence exists that the owners of Crystal Beach were permitting non-Crystal Beach Line steamers to dock at Crystal Beach through 1925 from longer distance ports.

The steamer *Colonial*, bound for her homeport of Dunkirk, New York on August 30, 1925 was to take excursionists to Crystal Beach upon her arrival. The steamer never arrived in Dunkirk due to a fire that killed three of her crew. She was beached and eventually scrapped. Coincidentally, the *Colonial* was part of the Crystal Beach Line many years earlier when it sailed as the *Darius Cole*.

Following page: The hull of the Colonial, formerly the Darius Cole of the Crystal Beach Line, beached near Dunkirk, New York. The people beach combing add perspective to reveal the size of the steamers.

Courtesy of Harvey Holzworth.

State of Ohio

Steamer "State of Ohio" arriving at Crystal Beach, Canada.

Post card of the State of Ohio at Crystal Beach. Whether she was an official steamer of the Crystal Beach Line or a special charter is uncertain. Following page, the State of Ohio approaching a dock at an unidentified location.

When John Rebstock opened the Crystal Beach International Assembly, he anticipated success on such a scale that he announced that the steamer *State of New York* would join the Line to accommodate the additional demand for passage to Crystal Beach. Unfortunately, the *State of New York* was not needed, nor was the steamer *State of Ohio* that could be brought into service *"to accommodate the crowds longing to visit the Crystal Beach International Assembly."*

The post card at left is evidence that the *State of Ohio* visited Crystal Beach, but in what capacity remains a mystery. The pier in the post card is the second pier built at the resort after the Assembly ceased operations after 1896.

Long before she became the *State of Ohio,* she was the *City of Cleveland.* The Detroit Dry Dock Company built the steamer in 1880 for the Detroit & Cleveland Steam Navigation Co. Five years later the D & C Line renamed her *City of Alpena.* The C & B Line purchased the steamer in 1892; that is when she became the *State of Ohio.*

Reduced to barge in 1925 she became stranded while entering Lorain, Ohio in fog, on December 17, 1929.

State of Ohio at Toledo, Ohio.

Courtesy of Harvey Holzworth.

STEAMERS STATE OF NEW YORK AND STATE OF OHIO

Above: Post card of the State of New York and State of Ohio.

Pilgrim

Pilgrim is the first of five steamers with uncertain connections with the Crystal Beach Line. Constructed during 1891 in Buffalo by David Bell, the *Pilgrim* regularly provided service to the resorts on Grand Island, primarily Eagle Park and Sheenwater. The *Pilgrim* made trips to Crystal Beach only during the first week of May 1893 and 1894.

A minor fire on the *Pilgrim* in early June 1894 put her out of commission for a period of at least three weeks while significant portions of her decks were rebuilt.

The final Great Lakes enrollment of the *Pilgrim* indicates a transfer from Buffalo to Portland, Maine on June 22, 1896, sold to the Casco Bay Steamboat Company of Portland for $20,000. Eventually, the *Pilgrim* was destroyed by fire in Bayonne, New Jersey on March 27, 1937.

Author's collection.

Top: A post card of the Pilgrim in Portland, Maine. Above: At an unidentified location.

City of *Erie*

Perhaps the most ornate steamer, at least on the interior, to cruise to Crystal Beach was the *City of Erie*. The Detroit Dry Dock Company built the *City of Erie* for the C & B Line in 1898 to handle increasing passenger traffic between Buffalo and Cleveland. Outfitted with 163 staterooms, the steamer was particularly popular with newlyweds on their way to Niagara Falls, and thus earned the name "Honeymoon Special." Eventually taken out of service, the steamer lay idle at Cleveland between 1937 and 1941. Then the Otis Steel Company purchased her for scrap.

The *City of Erie* is best known in maritime circles for narrowly winning a race with another steamer, the *Tashmoo* - both designed by Frank Kirby - a marine architect whose designs were perhaps the most prolific on the Great Lakes.

On August 8, 1908, the *City of Erie* stopped at Crystal Beach. It was the same day the park hosted the annual St. Andrews Scottish Society Picnic. The picnic's athletic games drew competitors and spectators from cities as far away as Cleveland and Detroit. Therefore, her Crystal Beach voyage may have been a special excursion by the C & B Line from west Lake Erie ports in connection with the games.

The announcement about the games only notes that the *Americana, Ossifrage*, and the *City of Erie* would sail to Crystal Beach on Saturday, August 8, 1908. The origin of the *City of Erie*'s Crystal Beach excursion is not clear.

Right, the interior of the City of Erie is perhaps the most elegant of all the steamers that ever docked at the Crystal Beach pier.

Eldorado

The Sloan and Cowles Company launched the *Eldorado* in Black Rock for the Grand Island trade, primarily to Sour Spring Grove.

In comparison to other lake and river steamers, the *Eldorado* must have looked like a bathtub toy. It was only 73 feet long and seventeen feet wide. She looked top-heavy and likely to capsize if struck broadside by a sudden, severe gust. She certainly would not have been able to handle rough seas on Lake Erie. Her exposure to such extreme conditions would have been rare given her regular sailing route, the Black Rock Canal and the channels of the Niagara River.

The seemingly top-heavy Eldorado loaded with excursions most likely heading for a Grand Island resort.

Returning from Crystal Beach, the *Eldorado* ran aground on "Gingerbread Reef" in 1893 which forced her into dry dock for repairs.

Eldorado eventually worked some trade routes on the cost of Maine and burned December 16, 1908 at Phippsburg.

Columbia

*I*ts unlikely that *Columbia* was part of the Crystal Beach Line, but she did offer round-trip excursions to Crystal Beach during 1894 for 10 cents. There was a mid-afternoon excursion and another at 8:15 PM every Thursday, Friday and Saturday. The evening excursions included music for dancing. She never docked at the Crystal Beach pier, only sailed into Point Abino Bay then returned to Buffalo.

Built in Buffalo by W. Murphy for James E. Conlon in 1892, the *Columbia* was not associated with any of the Niagara Frontier resorts. She frequently sailed

An ink drawing of the Columbia from the Buffalo Courier Record, May 23, 1897.

to Dunkirk, New York and Port Colborne, Ontario, and found business wherever she could, sometimes filling in for other steamers during breakdowns or days of high volume.

Its possible that her lack of direct affiliation with any of the local resorts precipitated her short history on the Niagara Frontier. In 1899, Hiram W. Sibley of Rochester purchased *Columbia* and converted her to a steam yacht and renamed it *Thetis*.

CHAPTER 4 *Steamers*
of the Lake Erie Excursion Company

Front page news about the impending sale of Crystal Beach in 1906 indicates that the Crystal Beach Steamboat and Ferry Company and the Lake Erie Excursion Company were partners in the enterprise which was about to be sold to the Detroit and Buffalo Line. This article was a smoke screen to hide the fact that owners of the Cleveland and Buffalo Transit Company were to become major investors in the LEEC and the LEEC, would then buy out its partner, the CBSFC.

The secretary of the Cleveland and Buffalo Transit Company, A.T. Zillmer, notes that C & B Line agent Harry S. Fisher (also a major stockholder of the LEEC) suggested to the C & B officers that it would be advantageous for the C & B Line to acquire the Crystal Beach operation. The C & B Line declined the opportunity, however, many of its officers expressed interest in the Lake Erie Excursion Company. The new investors would infuse the company with cash contingent upon an agreement that their dollars be used improve the park and for the construction two new steamers. Zillmer himself would become one of the investors that infused the LEEC with cash.

The Crystal Beach Line reached its zenith under the Lake Erie Excursion Company and the parade of steamers that comprised the Crystal Beach Line came to an end after the 1909 season. In 1910, the Buffalo Dry Dock Company launched the second of two palatial steamers ordered by the LEEC for the Line.

The first of these two steamers was American Ship Building Company "Steamer No. 213," according to their blue prints dated December 24, 1907. The first indication of her construction appeared in March 1907 in an announcement of the seasonal improvements for the upcoming summer season. *"Negotiations are now pending for the purchase of a boat which will be much speedier than any boat the company has ever had on the line."* The article implies that this new steamer would be ready for the 1908 season, as three steamers for 1907 were already under contract.

Americana

The American Shipbuilding Company received a contract from the Lake Erie Excursion Company for the construction of a new steamer capable of carrying more passengers during a single trip than all the steamers leased for the Crystal Beach Line during any of the previous seasons. Frank Kirby, prolific designer of Great Lakes steamers, based the Americana on an earlier vessel. Kirby stated that designing the steamer was no experiment, and *"She is built along the same lines as the Columbia* that has been on an 18-mile run out of Detroit for six years. I sharpened up the Americana some, as she is likely to encounter more sea here than the Columbia does on her run."*

The Buffalo Dry Dock Company, a unit of the American Shipbuilding Company, would build the steamer, referred to as Steamer 213 on the blue prints. Its hull had the distinction of being the first built with steel rolled at a new steel plant in Lackawanna.

*Different from the Columbia on page 99.

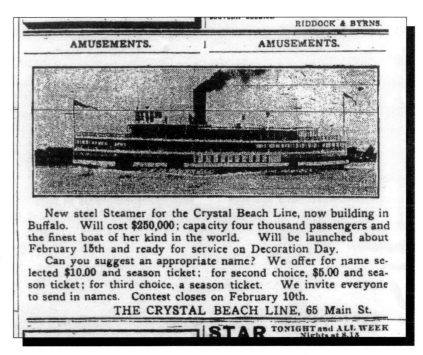

RIDDOCK & BYRNS.

AMUSEMENTS. | AMUSEMENTS.

New steel Steamer for the Crystal Beach Line, now building in Buffalo. Will cost $250,000; capacity four thousand passengers and the finest boat of her kind in the world. Will be launched about February 15th and ready for service on Decoration Day.

Can you suggest an appropriate name? We offer for name selected $10.00 and season ticket; for second choice, $5.00 and season ticket; for third choice, a season ticket. We invite everyone to send in names. Contest closes on February 10th.

THE CRYSTAL BEACH LINE, 65 Main St.

STAR TONIGHT and ALL WEEK Nights at 8.15

Ad for the "Name the new steamer of the Crystal Beach Line" contest, from the Buffalo Express, February 5, 1908. The steamer in the photo closely resembles the Americana, was probably Frank Kirby's Columbia.

On the following pages: It was cold and icy at the Buffalo Dry Dock Company on Ganson Street on February 22, 1908 with Hull 213 propped up just before her launch - from the collection of Cathy Herbert. Followed by a close-up of the prow of Hull 213 surrounded by dignitaries during the christening.

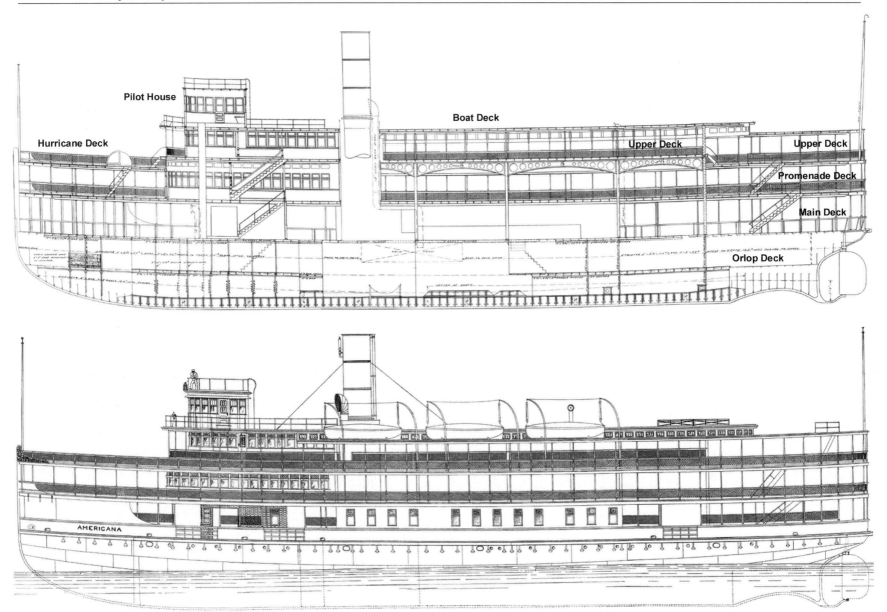

Prints courtesy of Historical Collections of the Great Lakes, Bowling Green State University. Digitally enhanced.

Orlop Deck

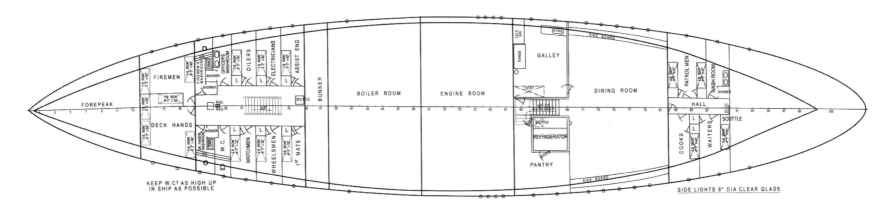

Main Deck

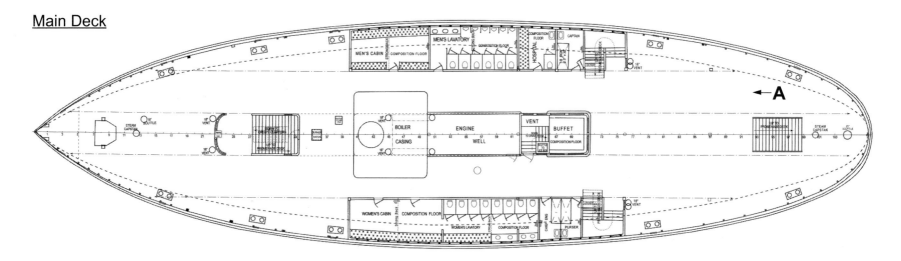

Prints courtesy of Historical Collections of the Great Lakes, Bowling Green State University.
Digitally redrawn. See Appendix Images for enlarged, split images of the floor plans.

Promenade Deck

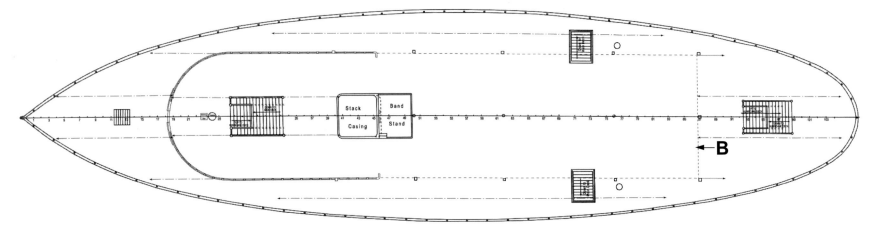

Hurricane/Third Deck

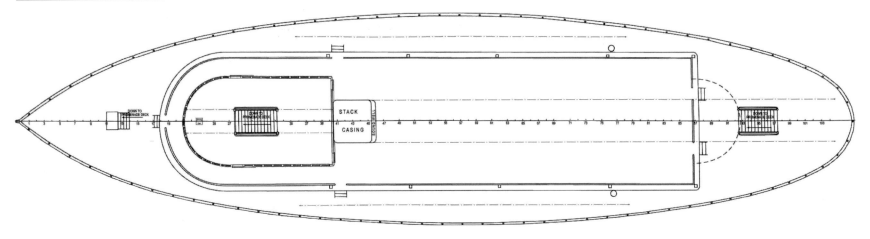

Prints courtesy of Historical Collections of the Great Lakes, Bowling Green State University.
Digitally redrawn. See Appendix Images for enlarged, split images of the floor plans.

Boat Deck

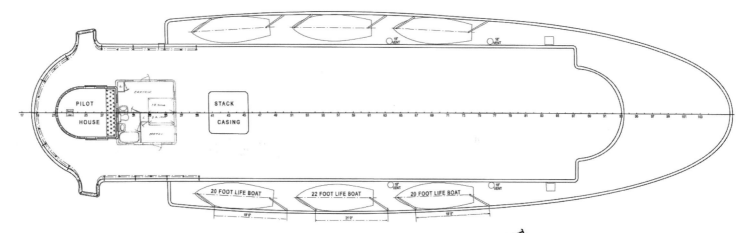

Note the Captain's and 1st Mates' quarters behind the pilot house (enlarged right). These quarters were not on the print at the time of Americana's construction, but were sketched onto the print at some point afterward. The year the sketch was drawn and then built behind Americana's pilot house is uncertain.

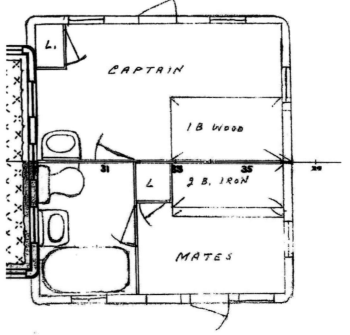

Prints courtesy of Historical Collections of the Great Lakes, Bowling Green State University. Digitally redrawn. See Appendix Images for enlarged, split images of the floor plans.

At the time of the *Americana's* launch, the Lake Erie Excursion Company announced that George S. Riley would be her first captain. Riley was already familiar with the Crystal Beach Line having served as first mate on the *Darius Cole*, then as first mate on the *State of New York*. Afterward he was elevated to the position of commander of *White Star*, then as master on the *State of New York* which made him one of the youngest masters on the Great Lakes.

George S. Riley - *Americana's* first master. Photo from the Buffalo Courier, February 23. 1908. (See Appendix Images for another photo.)

Page 108: Sliding sideways down heavily greased planks, Hull 213 hits the surface of the water creating a mini tsunami. At this time, Hull 213 became the Americana - the name submitted by E. P. Peugeot. Page 109: Americana afloat in the flooded drydock. The curving arch of the melted snow on the bank off her starboard side indicates how far the wave surged during the launch.

Work on the *Americana* would proceed at a brisk pace to have her completed in time for the Decoration Day opening of the park. The remaining superstructure and her three decks and the pilot house had to be constructed. Boilers, exhaust systems, miles of electrical cable, navigation equipment, plumbing - which included an ice-chilled drinking water system, all needed installation. The thousands of board feet of mahogany and oak for the interior of the steamer required hand carving, sanding, installation and finishing. Other surfaces and the entire exterior would need painting. There was less than three months to complete all this and more before her sea trials.

By mid May, the pristine *Americana* was the pride of the Buffalo Harbor, her white exterior and polished brass fixtures were blinding in bright sunlight. When Captain Riley sailed her from the Buffalo Dry Dock Company for the first time on May 18, 1908 for her sea trials, a chorus of steam whistles from other vessels in the harbor saluted her. Beyond the outer harbor walls, in the wide-open expanse of Lake Erie, her sea trials began. Her equipment was tested and her performance judged through a series of maneuvers and speed and directional changes. Her performance was outstanding. There was no question of her seaworthiness.

After the *Americana's* shakedown, the Lake Erie Excursion Company's Transportation Manager, F. J. Horagan, mailed invitations for the gala event of her trial run to Crystal Beach on May 27.

Ideal Weather conditions were on hand for *"Americana's Coming Out Party."* The ship's crew was *"as sharp as any that could be found on the finest ocean liners, greeting and tending to the guests and their duties in dress blues and gold braid."* Over 3,000 guests strolled the *Americana's* decks and cabins or danced on promenade deck.

Music composer and publisher A. Irving Talis. From the Buffalo Enquirer, May 28, 1908.

To commemorate the *Americana's* first run to Crystal Beach, the band played a waltz written by A. Irving Tallis, a Buffalo music publisher. Souvenir copies of the sheet music were presented the woman on board.

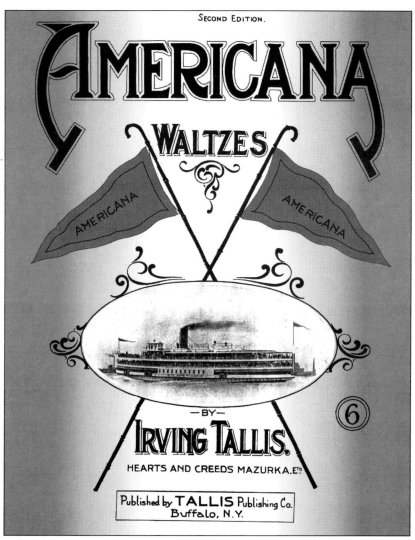

Digitally enhanced reproduction from the Author's collection.

Canoeists Russell Kief and Earl Zohn departed Crystal Beach at 5:30 PM on July 7, 1913 after a week-long canoe trip into Canada. A mile off shore, they realized that the strong winds churning up the lake would make a lake crossing to Buffalo impossible. Kief and Zohn tried to paddle back to the Beach, but the wind continued to blow them farther out. They decided to paddle along with the wind and make another attempt to land at Erie Beach where they could use the wind to their advantage. Conditions worsened as they paddled, and waves started to swamp the canoe.

Commanding the *Americana*, Captain Alfred Johnson spotted the two men clinging to their overturned canoe. He initiated life saving procedures that were ultimately successful, but did not go smoothly. A lifeboat manned by four crew members and a volunteer, smashed hard against the side of the *Americana* while being lowered. Damaged, the crew raised it back to the boat deck and the would-be rescuers boarded a second lifeboat. Raised off the boat deck, the ropes snapped before it could be positioned over the side and lowered. Deckhands lowered a third lifeboat into the water empty and the rescuers jumped into it from the *Americana's* lower deck.

The *Canadiana,* which had just started on a 3-hour cruise, departed from her regular course when her captain noticed the activity. He brought the steamer up broadside to the rescue in case her crew could be of assistance. Her presence worsened the situation when the wake from her propeller nearly capsized the lifeboat from her sister ship.

Eventually Kief and Zohn were safely in the lifeboat. Because of the rough seas, it would be impossible for the lifeboat to get close enough to the Americana without it smashing against the hull and

Americana departing Buffalo.

Previous page: A rare photo of the Americana's Main Deck salon photographed from location "A" on the floor plan on page 105. The diagonally sloped section of the ceiling on the right side of the photo is from the stairway to the Promenade Deck and is clearly indicated on the floor plan. All of the Canadiana's stairways ran bow to stern not side to side and did not have this ceiling feature. Note the beveled and leaded glass of the center buffet counter. Photo from the collection of Cathy Herbert.

tossing all the lifeboat's occupants into the lake before deckhands could fasten lines to it to raise it. So the *Americana* towed the lifeboat with a 500-foot rope - the length of which would minimize the effects of the *Americana's* motion in the rough water. From the decks of the *Americana*, the lifeboat came in and out of view. One instant it was at the crest of a wave, a moment later it was out of sight behind it as the steamer towed her rescued to the safety of Buffalo's harbor.

STEAMER AMERICANA, CRYSTAL BEACH LINE

Author's collection.

Exceptionally long, cold winters are not uncommon on the Niagara Frontier. The winter of 1925-26 must have been such a winter and followed by a spring that was slow to warm. The 1926 season at Crystal Beach opened on May 26 and ice still lined the shores of Lake Erie. In Point Abino Bay, there remained so much pack ice that the *Americana* could not dock at the pier.

Six days later, June 1, the *Americana* left her Buffalo dock to make another first run attempt to the park. Beyond the harbor walls, thick fog generated by warm air blown across the ice flows moving slowly eastward toward the Niagara River, shrouded the steamer. It forced her to proceed slowly. The *Americana* struck a number of large ice cakes in the flows and the impact, according to some passengers, caused the ship to rock. The ice field had gotten so thick that the trip was aborted.

Later that day, George Hall sailed to Crystal Beach in a tug to examine the ice conditions and reported that the ice was no longer tightly packed and melting rapidly. Conditions had improved considerably, but he decided not to send the *Americana* out.

"We found the ice going fast and it probably will all disappear within a matter of a few days," Hall said. *"We are guarding the safety of the beach patrons. Of course, we are sorry to disappoint the thousands anxious for the first boat ride of the season."*

Hall commented on the Memorial Day attendance, *"Hundreds made the trip by automobile and found the beach attractions in full swing. The picture offered by the ice in the lake on Memorial Day also provided an attraction in itself."* Those who traveled by auto came across the Niagara via ferries. The *Americana* resumed service the following day.

Crystal Beach advertisement noting the ice conditions on Lake Erie. Buffalo Courier Express, June 2, 1926.

Following page: Crystal Beach in winter circa 1970 surrounded by ice.

The *Americana* sailed between Buffalo and Crystal Beach for 21 seasons. Amazingly, after two decades of transporting millions, her history on the Crystal Beach Line is unremarkable. Her ending days with the Line began on August 18, 1925 when groundbreaking ceremonies marked the start of construction on the Peace Bridge, which opened in 1927.

By 1929, the Peace Bridge had cut dramatically into the ridership of the Crystal Beach Line. The *Americana* was sold to Meseck Line in New York City and put into service ferrying people between Battery Park in Lower Manhattan to Rye Beach - another summer/amusement resort - north of New York City. Her journey there was more tempestuous than all her years on the Crystal Beach Line.

At that time, the *Americana* was too wide for the Welland and St. Lawrence locks. To facilitate her journey to downstate New York, her three decks were cut at the hull line, folded inward and secured with cables tied from side to side. Additionally, the hull had to be bent four inches inward. To accomplish this, the steel plates were heated and pulled toward the center of the ship with turnbuckles. Upon arrival at Montreal, the hull was jacked back out and the decks turned back down, secured and repaired. She then departed for New York City - it was November 16, 1929. Captain Alfred Johnson was the last Captain of the *Americana* for the Crystal Beach Line, commanding her from Buffalo to Montreal where her new owners accepted delivery.

Left: Americana at the Main Street dock.

Americana with her decks folded upward just before her cruise through the Welland Canal and to her new home in New York City. The inset is an enlargement of the Main Deck showing the exposed water closets of the women's restroom.

Courtesy of the Milwaukee Public Library, Great Lakes Marine Collection.

The Americana before her one way cruise to New York City. Note her exposed lower deck that normally is enclosed and extends beyond her hull.

The Americana with her decks reassembled and her main deck completely open, sporting a new paint job. Directly behind the wheel house is the extension of the pilot house added some years after her launch. It is more visible in the photo on page 118.

Only one day out of Montreal, she lost both of her anchors in the Bay of Fundy during a storm that sent her back to port. The second day out, she ran for twenty-four hours against severe headwinds and progressed only ten miles. After five days, she docked at Canso, Nova Scotia for undisclosed repairs. Afterward, her crew reported spotting a whale, a seal, but most of the time there was ice. The *Americana* reached Boston around December 17, and finally reached New York City on December 20, 1929. A journey that normally would have taken five days took over a month.

On July 12, 1938, the *Americana* was back in the Buffalo newspapers. While returning to Newark, New Jersey from Roton Point, Connecticut she ran aground on mud flats while entering the Newark harbor at 12:30 AM. A fireboat and several tugs freed her. She docked without damage or injury to her passengers.

Author's collection.

Courtesy of Westchester County/Rye Playland.

Above: The Americana at Rye Playland, 1930. Photo: Left: The Americana was the pride of the Meseck Line, and featured in the Line's 1939 brochure for Playland at Rye Beach and the World's Fair in New York. The Meseck Line operated four steamers, the S.S. Richard Peck - capacity 2,500; the S.S. Winchester - capacity 2,000; the S.S. Wauketa - capacity 1,300; and the S.S. Americana - capacity 3,500. Her route had changed, but its primary port of call was Rye Playland - an amusement park and beach. Moonlight and Sunday cruises remained a specialty with free dancing on "the Finest and Largest Maple Wood Dance Floors Afloat." A route map of the Meseck Line fleet, including the Americana, can be found in the Appendix, Table 2.

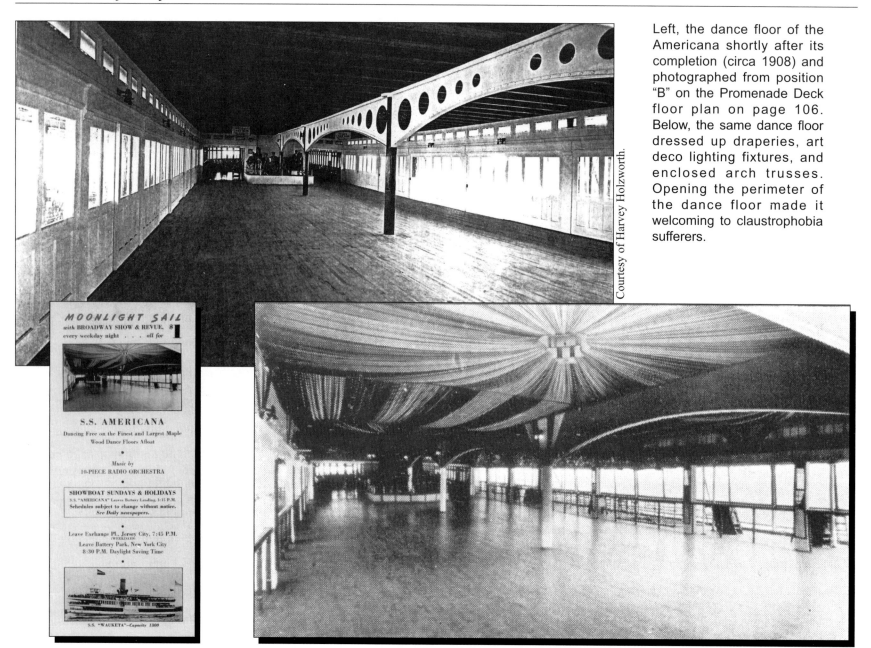

Courtesy of Harvey Holzworth.

Left, the dance floor of the Americana shortly after its completion (circa 1908) and photographed from position "B" on the Promenade Deck floor plan on page 106. Below, the same dance floor dressed up draperies, art deco lighting fixtures, and enclosed arch trusses. Opening the perimeter of the dance floor made it welcoming to claustrophobia sufferers.

The steamers City of Keansburg and Americana at the Battery on July 20, 1952.

Courtesy of the Steamship Historical Society of America.

Roton Point Association.

Left: The Americana, closest to the dock at Roton Point - another waterfront resort with a beach, dance hall, rides and coasters.

Following page: The Americana sailing up the East River en-route to Rye Beach or other stops on the Meseck Line route, her back half shadowed by the bridge. Manhattan in the background.

The Crystal Beach Line is rumored to have overloaded her steamers on occasion - particularly on exceptionally busy return trips late at night when the probability of scrutiny by a harbor master would be minimal. There is no official evidence of overloading. No fines were levied, no citations issued. No legal action was ever taken against the Line or the masters of her vessels. Harry Daugherty of the Meseck Line, and Captain of the Americana was not as lucky as the Crystal Beach Line captains.

The Merchant Marine Division of the U.S. Coast Guard suspended Daugherty's license on August 6, 1944 following a hearing on a number of charges against him. They found Daugherty guilty of overloading, failure to keep an accurate count of passengers in the ship's log, and registering an incorrect number of passengers in the

log on three occasions. The Coast Guard also referred the matter to the U.S. attorney because overloading a vessel may have involved violating federal statutes.

On the Meseck Line, the Americana's official capacity had been reduced substantially from 3,500 on the Crystal Beach Line to 2,700. The Coast Guard did not disclose the number of passengers Daugherty boarded on each of the three infractions.

Right up until her last excursions to Rye Beach in 1953, the Americana also provided excursions up the Hudson River though most of her time was spent on the East River and Long Island Sound.

The *Americana* eventually succumbed to age, declining patronage and changing times. She was taken to Baltimore, Maryland and scrapped during October 1953.

Courtesy of Rick Doan.

Canadiana

Every aspect of the *Americana's* launch was a dress rehearsal for the launch of the *"Americana II"* - as the vessel was dubbed during her construction. She was a near duplicate of the *Americana*. Only a keen observer would be able to spot the exterior differences - the most prominent one was the captain's quarters built directly behind the pilot house - which eventually became less prominent once the same feature was added to *Americana's* pilot house. She was built from *Americana's* blue prints and affected only by minor changes to the deck plans, most of them to the crew's quarters on the Orlop deck. The festivities surrounding the launch of the *Americana II* were also duplicated including the "Name the New Steamer" contest. The Captain and Chief Engineer were the same (their commissions transferred to the new ship from the Americana); the luminaries present for the *American's* launch were nearly identical.

The *Americana II,* or "Hull 215," was launched from the Buffalo Dry Dock facilities on March 5, 1910.

When her hull and partially completed superstructure slid down greased timbers into the canal at the Buffalo Dry Dock Company, a flag unfurled announcing her name, *"Canadiana."*

The *Canadiana's* new engine was in the hold on the freighter Mary H. Boyce. In order to keep the *Canadiana's* build-out on schedule, the freighter forced her way through unbroken ice in the harbor to deliver the engine to the Buffalo Dry Dock Company.

Already a proven vessel given the performance of the *Americana*, the *Canadiana* performed flawlessly during her sea trials on June 11, 1910. Her inaugural voyage to Crystal Beach, guests by invitation only, took place on June 30, 1910. Again, Irving Tallis published a song to commemorate the occasion, "The Canadiana March." She officially began her long commission on July 2, 1910, marking the beginning of Crystal Beach's golden era.

Left, The Canadiana during an evening docking at Crystal Beach.

THE LAUNCHING OF THE CANADIANA.

Photos of Canadiana's launch are rare. These three grainy images of her launch early in March 1910 reveal milder weather compared to the day her sister was launched. The photo of her striking the water mirrored on the water's surface is exceptional in spite of the grain. Ms. Carmilla M. Boland submitted the winning entry in the contest to name the steamer.

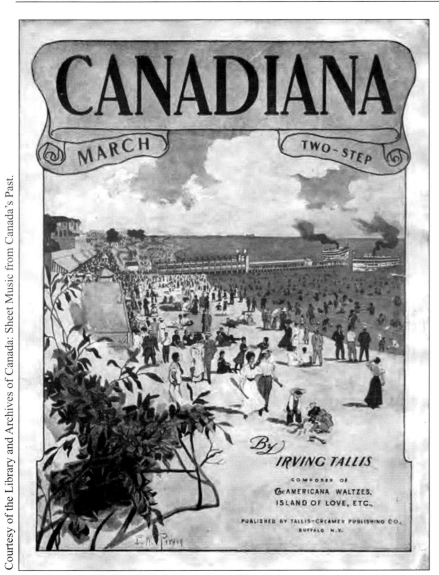

Front page of Irving Tallis' Canadiana March.

Top: S.S. Canadiana departing on mer maiden voyage in 1910.
Above: Heading out of Buffalo during the 1950s.

Orlop Deck

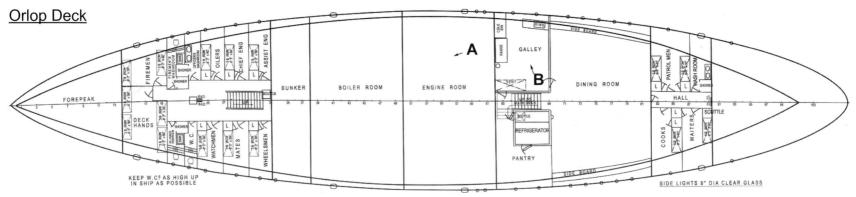

Print courtesy of Historical Collections of the Great Lakes, Bowling Green State University.
Digitally redrawn. See Appendix Images for enlarged, split images of the floor plans.

Previous page: A triple expansion steam engine propelled the Canadiana (position "A" on the Orlop Deck floor plan above). The steamer Mary H. Boyce (above) delivered the engine to the Buffalo Dry Dock Company. The Canadiana's boilers were changed from coal burning to oil before the 1951 season. The conversion was done by the Oldman Boiler Works at a cost of $43,000. Left, the galley as seen from position "B" on the Orlop Deck plan. The sign in the galley warns that nothing be thrown overboard while at the beach. Right: The crews quarters were all tight, but a room with two bunks indicate it was occupied low ranking officers. Bunks of deck hands were 3-tiered.

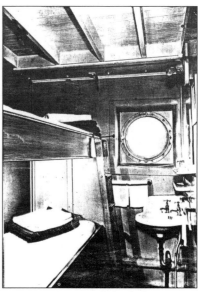

Courtesy of Harvey Holzworth.

Main Deck

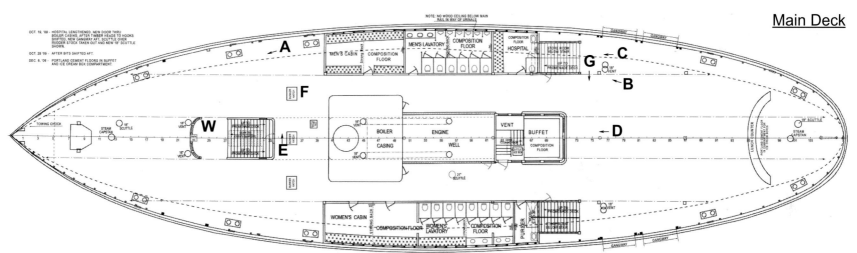

Print courtesy of Historical Collections of the Great Lakes, Bowling Green State University. Digitally redrawn. See Appendix Images for enlarged, split images of the floor plans.

Courtesy of Rick Doan.

Right: The starboard staircase photographed from position "B" on the plan for the Main Deck above.

Previous page: Looking into the bow as seen from position "A" on the Main Deck floor plan above. Roped off, this area is being used for storage. The woman at the far left in the photo is standing at the base of the stairway to the Promenade Deck (W above).

Courtesy of Cathy Herbert.

Left: The refreshment and snack bar on the Main Deck. photographed from position "D" on the floor plan on the previous page.

Below: Another view of the starboard side stair case. The refreshment and snack bar to the left. Photographed from position "C" on the floor plan on the previous page.

Courtesy of Cathy Herbert.

CRYSTAL BEACH TRANSIT CO.,
3 HOUR LAKE RIDE
BUFFALO to
CRYSTAL BEACH
AND RETURN
1956
GOOD ONLY THIS SEASON   Form UL
001111

Author's collection.

Courtesy of Harvey Holzworth.

Courtesy of Harvey Holzworth.

Courtesy of Cathy Herbert.

Above: Unidentified men at the refreshment and snack bar photographed from position "G."

Right: With the aide of motorized wheel barrows, men load coal onto the Canadiana. They are dumping it through the deck hatch where the coal sits on the floor and located in position "F" on the Main Deck floor plan on page 133. Photographed from position "E."

The "Name the Steamer" contests and open invitations extended to everyone through the newspapers to come aboard and inspect the steamers before their commissions began were masterful strokes of public relations by The Lake Erie Excursion Company. They gave Buffalonians a sense of pride in the vessels as if they were their own.

Many of the photos of the *Canadiana's* interior that appear in this book were photographed after she had been in operation for a very long time. Wear and age to the appointments are evident, but the quality and detail of the craftsmanship remain.

Looking up the Grand Staircase to the third deck cabin. Note the intricate globe on the lamp post. This photo was taken from position "A" on the Promenade Deck floor plan on the following page.

Promenade Deck

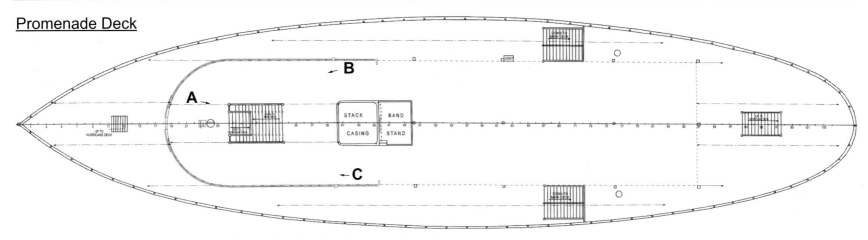

Print courtesy of Historical Collections of the Great Lakes, Bowling Green State University.
Digitally redrawn. See Appendix Images for enlarged, split images of the floor plans.

Two more views of the Promenade Deck cabin and the Grand Staircase, taken from positions "B" and "C" respectively on the deck floor plan above. Note the stained glass near the ceiling above the the windows.   Courtesy of the Lower lakes Marine Historical Society and Harvey Holzworth.

Promenade Deck

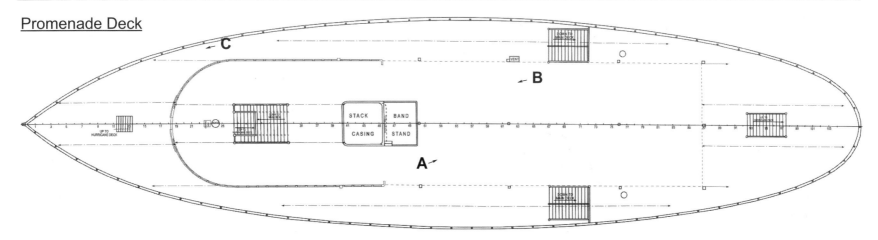

Print courtesy of Historical Collections of the Great Lakes,
Bowling Green State University.
Digitally redrawn. See Appendix Images for enlarged, split images of the floor plans.

Previous page: A 1950s view across the dance floor to the stern, from position "A" on the Promenade Deck plan above. At right, a crowd surrounding the stage, photographed from position "B." Below: The crowd surges down the pier to customs and the park entrance, photographed from "C."

Courtesy of Cathy Herbert.

The view from position "A" on the Upper Deck plan on the following page. Notice the raised portion of the deck where, underneath is the dance floor on the Promenade Deck.

Looking down the Grand Staircase from the Upper Deck from position "B."

Hurricane/Third Deck

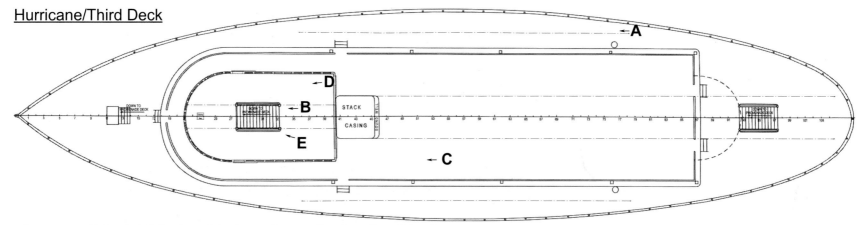

Print courtesy of Historical Collections of the Great Lakes, Bowling Green State University.
Digitally redrawn. See Appendix Images for enlarged, split images of the floor plans.

Courtesy of Cathy Herbert.

Above: Looking along the port side toward the bow from position "C" on the Upper Deck plan. The counter behind the row of chairs was added later and not on the original print. The door opens into the third deck cabin and the Grand Staircase down to the Promenade Deck. The ladder provides access to the Boat Deck, Pilot House and the Captain's quarters.

Right: The Hurricane Deck's cabin photographed from position "D." The linoleum is not original.

Life boat drills on the boat deck. The larger photo was taken midship facing the bow, the inset facing the stern (positions "A" and "B" on the Boat Deck plan on the following page). Note the Skyway under construction in the inset photo.

Boat Deck

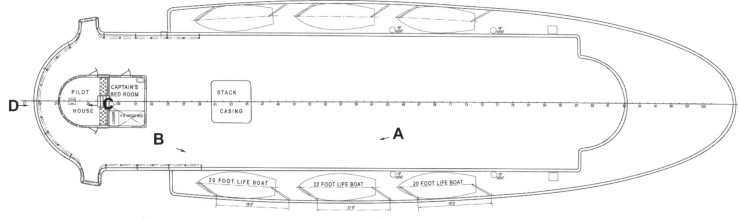

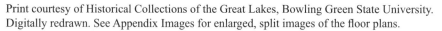

Print courtesy of Historical Collections of the Great Lakes, Bowling Green State University. Digitally redrawn. See Appendix Images for enlarged, split images of the floor plans.

Above: The wheel as seen from the door from the Captain's Quarters. Right, the Pilot House from the bow of the Hurricane Deck. Position "C" and "D" on the Boat Deck floor plan above.

Above: Aerial of the Buffalo Dry Dock Company and the Canadiana in dry dock, circa 1940.

Men at work on the Canadiana's prop from ground level.

Both photos courtesy of the Lower lakes Marine Historical Society and Harvey Holzworth.

Working on the prop, photographed from the dry dock floor.

As World War II escalated, so did rationing in the United States and Canada. To conserve oil, gasoline and rubber, unnecessary automobile travel was discouraged. By 1943, there was a ban against driving for "pleasure" purposes. There were checks at strategic points along the lakeshore roads, near golf courses and at the Peace Bridge. Advertisements encouraged patrons to save gasoline and rubber, and take the *Canadiana* to Crystal Beach.

Above: Chryslers delivered to Buffalo by ship fill a staging area of the Lackawanna Railroad before driven caravan-style to regional dealers. The railroad let the Crystal Beach Line use this area for a parking lot for the Line's Commercial Street dock in the background. The white building houses the ticket office; it is the same building in front of the Canadiana in the photo at left.

Left: At the time of this photo, circa 1920, driving to Crystal Beach was not an option for the sea of people jammed at the dock. Most of them would have to wait for another boat - not uncommon during Crystal Beach's hey day. Safety was a concern during such times because the people had to cross railroad tracks to reach the Canadiana and often, the crowd extended beyond the tracks. Eventually, a tunnel under the tracks ameliorated the safety issues.

Above: The dock area as seen from where the man is leaning against the rail at the bottom of the ramp in the photo at left.

Author's collection.

Instructions inside this matchbook cover indicate that it, along with 15 cents was redeemable for a ride on the Cyclone, Giant Coaster or Laff in the Dark.

An incident during the mid afternoon of June 19, 1943 had all the ingredients of an Irwin Allen disaster epic. The *Canadiana* was on its 3:00 PM run to the park and her decks were full of people enjoying a sunny day and lake breezes. When the steamer was off Windmill Point, first officer Thomas Fagen turned his head skyward toward the sound of a Royal Canadian Air Force (RCAF) Harvard training plane.

The passengers on board were treated to an unexpected air show when the pilot of the plane began stunt flying very close to the steamer. It buzzed overhead during crossings earlier in the day and numerous other times during the past week. This time the pilot was flying exceptionally low and very close to the steamer. Fagen swore that the plane would clip the flagpole of the steamer.

"A couple of times, we thought he was trying to knock off our flagpole. That plane or a similar one had been doing stunts around the steamer several times during the day and often during the last week"

- Thomas Fagen
First Officer
Canadiana

1: The silhouette is of a girl on the Canadiana watching the Harvard Trainer approach the steamer at low altitude.

Left: The Ontario shore of Lake Erie showing Windmill Point.

Photos 1,3,5,6: Henry Golaszewski, from the Buffalo Courier Express, June 21, 1943. Photo 2: Arthur Orlowski, from the Buffalo Evening News, June 21, 1943. Photo 4: Arthur Stubbs, from the Buffalo Evening News, June 21, 1943. Lower Lakes Marine Historical Society news clippings scrap books.

Frank Dimond, one of the *Canadiana's* watchmen also had his eyes on the trainer as it circled the ship several times just above the surface of the lake. The plane was between 75 and 100 feet away from the steamer when it started to rise then suddenly drop to hit the water with the sound of a cannon. The passengers could see the wings being ripped from the fuselage as the plane made contact with the water with a huge splash. Then the plane went under. The crash occurred at 3:25 PM.

The plane hit the water less than half the *Canadiana's* length away. Fortunately the plane did not bank toward the steamer before its sudden drop - at 75 to 100 feet the impact site was a near miss. Similarly, it is fortunate that parts of the disintegrating fuselage did not ricochet off the surface of the water and hit the ship.

"The plane had been flying around the boat for some time. Then it seemed to explode right over the boat, the motor died and the plane crashed into the lake a short distance away."

- Lieutenant Harold L. Simon
74th Regiment, U.S. Coast Guard
Canadiana Passenger

2: The Harvard Trainer photographed from the Canadiana as it swoops by. Note the silhouette of the pilot in the cockpit with the sliding glass cockpit cover open. 3: Seconds before the crash.

The *Canadiana* came about and deckhands lowered a lifeboat but the pilot never emerged and the only trace of the plane was a large oil slick.

The trainer crashed into water that was approximately 50 feet deep. A civil air patrol plane circled the area but even from the air, spotters could not see traces of the plane on the lake bottom.

Two launches from the U.S. Coast Guard started recovery efforts that continued into the night, aided by searchlights. At 12:30 AM on the morning of July 20, their grappling efforts recovered the cockpit of the trainer that held the body of the pilot. Both were turned over to Canadian authorities.

The plane originated from the Dunnville, Ontario RCAF Service Flying Training School 6 approximately 60 miles west of Buffalo. Pilot Trainee Leading Aircraftsman William Charles Smith was at the controls of the Harvard 2963 trainer. He is buried at Riverside Cemetary in Dunnville.

4: Just after impact and going down. 5: The plane's rudder just above the surface with a wing floating on the surface of the roiling water. 6: Sinking debris.

Right: The line about the Canadiana outline marks the 100 foot perimeter about the ship and the greater estimate of where the Harvard Trainer plane plunged into the lake - dangerously close, considering the distance is less than half the Canadiana's length away. See Appendix Table 7 for more information on the Harvard Trainer.

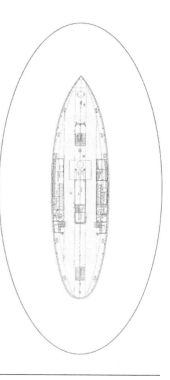

One - Armed Bandits

"George Hall Sr. ... maintained that the central area of the lake was the equivalent to the high seas; that out there they were in international waters ... the newspaper had no difficulty in pointing out that there was, in fact, just a line drawn in the water ... dividing the two countries. You are in one country or the other; never neither. The Buffalo police showed up at the boat the next day or two, with sledgehammers in hand, the slots were taken off and smashed to pieces on the dock."

- S.S. Canadiana History Book
Unpublished Manuscript
http://sscanadiana.org/begin.html

At the bottom of the staircase, three male teens are gathered around a slot machine.

There were slot machines on the *Canadiana*, but the year they first appeared is unknown. Their presence may date back as the early 1930s when the Buffalo and Crystal Beach Corporation (BCBC) went into bankruptcy. When the BCBC emerged from bankruptcy in part as the Crystal Beach Transit Company (CBTC), which operated the *Canadiana*, the slot machines may have been introduced to increase income.

Early in July of 1946, the National Education Association (NEA) held a convention in Buffalo and one of its delegates, along with a reporter from the Buffalo Courier Express boarded the *Canadiana*. Whether it was their intent to observe minors gambling on board or incidental to an excursion to the park is unknown. They observed teenagers vying with adults for positions at the machines that were locked and concealed while the ship was at the dock. Once the *Canadiana* was on its way, the slots opened and teens were dropping their change into them in spite of signs forbidding minors from playing. They noted a girl about 16 years old spend all of her money on a machine before the boat reached the park.

George C. Hall noted that the CBTC employed men whose job was to make change for the adults and prevent minors from playing the machines - yet the reporter and the NEA delegate observed such an employee make change for the girl and do nothing to stop her or the other minors.

Subsequent reports noted that raids on the *Canadiana* were imminent as the police commissioner sought council on the legality of boarding the steamer to seize the machines. The police intended the raid to be a warning to private clubs in the city where slot machines were in use.

The U.S. Attorney General informed the police commissioner that they may be able to seize the machines but would have trouble obtaining convictions on any state penal laws because of the federal licensing fees collected.

Police were informed by the CBTC on August 16, 1946, that the machines had been removed. The police warned that the steamer would be watched closely and arrests would follow any attempts to put them back on board.

A follow-up report in 1947 noted that an inspection of the *Canadiana* by police in July yielded no slot machines, nor did it make reference to an earlier raid and sledgehammer-wielding police. Confirmation of the police action above remains for additional research to discover.

The Canadiana at the Crystal Beach Pier on a quiet day at the park, circa 1940.

Courtesy of the Fort Erie Historical Museum

Not as dramatic perhaps, as the crew of *Americana* rescuing canoeists during a wind storm, the *Canadiana* came to the rescue of Mr. and Mrs. James Malonson and their cat as the 1951 season was winding down to a close. The trio had been stranded and floating adrift in the lake for over two hours after the engine in their 22-foot motor boat failed. They were three miles off the Canadian shore, and managed to attract the attention of the *Canadiana's* crew by constantly blowing their horn as the vessel approached. Captain Malloy ordered the ship to come to the side of the motor boat, and the couple and their cat where brought aboard with a rope ladder. Because of high seas, the *Canadiana* was unable to take the motorboat in tow. Once in Buffalo, however, the Coastguard was notified, and they managed to tow the stricken boat to port.

Aerial perspectives of the Canadiana and Crystal Beach. Top: at the "Second" pier circa 1920, Photo: Archives of Ontario. Above: at the "Third" Pier, circa 1950.Following pages: Slightly blurred, but nonetheless, beautiful shots of the Canadiana and Crystal Beach in the summer twilight.

Courtesy of the Archives of Ontario.

Courtesy of the Fort Erie Historical Museum.

A sad commentary on the social inequalities and discrimination during the 20th Century erupted in the form of riots at Crystal Beach - in the village and in the park on opening day, May 30, 1956. Later that evening, the disruptive gangs boarded the *Canadiana* for the 9:30 PM trip for Buffalo. During boarding, the Ontario Provincial Police repeatedly announced that fighting on board would not be tolerated. However, as soon as the steamer pulled away from the pier, the violence erupted starting with exploding firecrackers.

The rioting on board did not resemble a western movie barroom brawl with chairs breaking on backs, people falling off balconies and down staircases while bottles and glasses smashed into mirrors and shattered on walls with everyone throwing punches. However, wherever the gangs of black, angry teens prowled, there was fighting. There were some incidents where injuries were sustained from swinging beer bottles. Reportedly, the teens brandished switchblades, pushed and shoved people as they prowled the decks, some people were thrown down to the deck floors. Many suffered powder burns from exploding firecrackers. The crew began hiding many frightened and injured passengers in the ship's dining room and protected older passengers and their children by concealing them in the crew's quarters. The Orlop deck refugees could hear the stomping of running

feet and shouting from the roving gangs overhead. Three private policemen and the *Canadiana's* crew did their best to stop the violence, but as soon as they broke up one fight, another erupted elsewhere. They did manage to lock up some of the offenders.

Buffalo policemen armed with nightsticks greeted the *Canadiana* and placed three teenagers under arrest. Dozens of frightened and disheveled women exited the boat with stories of packs of teenagers roaming the decks and starting fights.

The CBTC announced it would increase the number of policemen on the Line from three to five. Fillmore Hall also emphasized the CBTC would exercise its right to refuse to sell boat tickets to any groups which appear troublesome. For the July 4th holiday, Hall said teenagers would not be allowed to board the *Canadiana* unless accompanied by a parent.

Attendance on the Line had been steadily decreasing. The Peace Bridge Authority reported the entries for 1950, 1951 and 1954 are indicative of the increasing volume of automobile travel. In spite of the Line's safety record, patronage never recovered to the fleeting pre-riot levels. On November 27, 1956, Fillmore Hall announced that the CBTC would no longer operate the 46 year-old steamer. According to Hall, increasing operating costs and decreasing patronage forced the decision, which,

Hall admitted, was not easy to reach. Long before this announcement, George C. Hall, in 1951, commented on the disappearing passenger trade on the Lakes, stating that the automobile and high cost of ship operations have all but killed it. He also pointed out that salaries of passenger ship crews have risen 300% in 12 years.

George Hall is reported to have said that they wanted to keep the Line operating, but to do so, they would need to cut its operating schedule, and salary to its crew proportionately. The union, however, insisted its *Canadiana* members be paid in full regardless of the schedule. Ultimately because of the union's inflexibility on salary, the CBTC ceased operating the Line.

It is impossible to ascertain whether the *Canadiana* would have operated beyond 1956 if the riots had not precipitated fear that further reduced its patronage. Although the riot was not the ultimate reason for terminating operations, it did have a role.

A police paddy wagon accompanied by a number of the Buffalo police wait for the Canadiana to dock. All of this was largely for show as there were no further incidents of rioting after May 30, 1956.

Two Ladies Leaping

On August 1, 1929, Alice LaRoque, on her way home to Buffalo after an overnight stay at Crystal Beach, suddenly walked to the bow of the *Canadiana*, took off her shoes, and jumped overboard from the Promenade Deck - a fall of approximately 20 feet. A week later, fishermen discovered her body floating in the lake off Windmill Point.

Its improbable that investigators or newspapers conducted any in-depth investigations into an obvious suicide, especially since Alice was virtually penniless and a relative newcomer to the Niagara Frontier. No suicide note was ever recovered (or reported).

Details about her background are sketchy. She came to Buffalo from New Orleans two years earlier and she was 21 years old at the time of her death. She had difficulty holding down a job and was currently unemployed. Just before departing for Crystal Beach, Alice informed the matron of the St. Rose of Lima Home that she was going there to look for work.

Acquaintances of Alice, Leo Steinberg and Emil Nyman, traveled with her that day. They spent the day

Author's collection.

The wake trail in front of the Canadiana indicates an afternoon departure from the Crystal Beach pier.

on the beach and the evening in the park. Reportedly, the young men spent the night with friends while Alice stayed at a rooming house.

The trio departed Crystal Beach on the 11:00 AM boat; the men were not with Alice when she jumped. They told Captain Wilcock that she seemed sad that morning and an argument with her boyfriend had upset her.

Its possible to construct a number of theories regarding the circumstances that compelled Alice to take her life by jumping from the *Canadiana's* bow, even from these meager details. It takes little imagination to construct a theory based on Alice's difficulties supporting herself, and the possibility that she was pregnant with her boyfriend's baby who refused support when she confronted him.

Alice is the only known fatality associated with the *Canadiana*; however, the steamer maintained an impeccable safety record.

Shortly after 7:00 P.M. on June 26, 1941, four men fishing from a motorboat on Lake Erie heard a distress signal coming from the *Canadiana*. When they looked up to the steamer, they saw Captain William Malloy trying to trying to get their attention, then pointing to a spot in the lake. The men in the motorboat learned that someone went overboard from the steamer.

The *Canadiana* did not have the ability to maneuver with the speed and efficiency of a motorboat, which is why Captain Malloy signaled to the men fishing when he heard someone shout, "Man overboard!" Even as Malloy signaled to the motorboat, the wheelman was turning the *Canadiana* about.

The four men in the motorboat* found 44 year old Mrs. Sarah Erlin floundering in the water, and pulled her to safety.

Meanwhile, men at the Coast Guard base also heard the distress signal and set out for the *Canadiana*. At the scene, the Coast Guard brought Sarah aboard their boat, then the *Canadiana* continued on her way to Buffalo.

The Coast Guard whisked Erlin to Buffalo and then to Columbus Hospital. She sustained no serious injuries.

Sarah had already made one round trip to Crystal

From the collection of Cathy Herbert

From the collection of Rick Doan.

*Benjamin F. Dailey (motorboat owner), William Keenan, Elmer Johnson, Anthony Radice - all of Buffalo.

From the collection of Rick Doan.

Beach earlier in the day, and she was about an eighth of a mile from home on the return leg of her second round trip when she went overboard. The nature of her trips remains a mystery. She did tell Chief Hugh F. Brown of the Coast Guard that she had gotten a dizzy spell and fell overboard. She told the patrolmen that took her to the hospital that some boys were playing and pushed her over the side.

Captain Malloy, however, reported a different story that indicates Mrs. Erlin had attempted suicide. A woman surrendered a purse to Malloy, and told him it belonged to Mrs. Erlin. This woman met Mrs. Erlin earlier, and asked that she give the purse to her [Erlin's] daughter.

Everyone involved may have learned more about Erlin's leap into the lake, but the truth remains a mystery.

A pensive Fillmore Hall just before the buttoned up Canadiana departs Buffalo in 1958 when she was leased for a commission between Toledo and Bob-Lo Island.

A Slow Death

Declining passenger trade on the Great Lakes is evident in the fact that there was no apparent interest in the *Canadiana* after she had been put up for sale, and she floated idle in Buffalo during 1957. In 1958, Seaway Excursion Lines leased the *Canadiana* for a three-year commission sailing between Cleveland, Ohio and Bob-Lo Island on the Canadian side of the Detroit River. The *Canadiana* arrived in Toledo on May 28, 1958 and began sailing to Bob-Lo two days later.

Two months into her commission, the *Canadiana* was following an ore boat in the Maumee River. A railroad swing bridge crossing the river had opened to let the ore boat pass and after it had, the bridge began to close. Signals from the *Canadiana* went unnoticed as the steamer was moving forward at less than half speed and unable to stop. Passengers ran toward the stern as the bridge crashed into the Hurricane and Promenade decks, collapsing them at the bow down onto the Main deck.

Debris from the Canadiana on the swinging span of the Toledo Terminal Railroad bridge.

Labor strife at the American Ship Building Company delayed the necessary repairs, and the *Canadiana* remained out of service for the remainder of the season, which effectively sunk the Seaway Excursion Lines. On August 7, 1958, the U.S. Federal Government seized the ship at the behest of the Maritime Trade Union. They sought the nearly $50,000 in back wages and vacation benefits for the *Canadiana's* 35 crew members that had not been paid since mid July.

The Crystal Beach Transit Company became the receivers of the Seaway Excursion Lines, and the Admiralty, for the Crystal Beach Transit Company along with 15 insurance companies* began preparing a suit against the railroad that owned the bridge.

Meanwhile, George Vizneau of the Toledo Excursion Lines was the successful bidder when *Canadiana* was auctioned on October 13, 1958. He paid $28,500 with a mortgage from the Lucas County Bank. Repairs to the *Canadiana* went forward with the rebuilding of the Promenade Deck - the bow left exposed to the open air. Instead of rebuilding the Hurricane Deck, stairs descended to the open air Promenade.

Heavy winter ice punctured the hull in February 1959. Taking on water; the *Canadiana* developed a 20-degree list before repairs were made.

She operated during the summer of 1959 and was

The shattered Hurricane and Promenade decks collapsed onto the Main Deck after the collision with the swinging railroad bridge.

*They were awarded $155,000 in November 1965, after a judge ruled that the damage to the Canadiana was the fault of the railroad.

seized shortly after by the U.S. Marshall for back wages and the unpaid mortgage. Lucas County Bank retained ownership of the steamer until November 1960 then sold it to the Pleasurama Excursion Lines of Cleveland, which unofficially changed her name to Pleasurama.

Pleasurama Excursion Lines and Cedar Point had big plans for the *Canadiana*. The park would run excursions from Cleveland four times a week. Pleasurama would demolish Cedar Point's old dock, and erect a new one while the Park would recondition the trams used to bring passengers from the dock to the middle of the park. The *Canadiana* was to receive a $90,000 renovation to include updated washrooms, installation of a 2,000-person dining

Above left: The damage removed and repairs underway. Left: Sailing again without the Hurricane Deck and the open air Promenade Deck at the bow.

room, a bar and cocktail lounge, and a children's play area. Plans also called for a new pilothouse and a modern-looking exhaust stack.

The renovations began at the Buffalo Dry Dock Company on July 15, 1962. Once in dry dock, workers enclosure of the Main Deck began, then the Buffalo Dry Dock Company closed and the renovations ceased.

Top: The Canadiana docked at the Buffalo Dry Dock Company as the smaller of the two docks, and most likely the one where she was built, is partially filled in following the American Ship Building Company's decision to close the facility. Above: The Canadiana back in Cleveland with her decks enclosed and looking neglected.

Removed from dry dock, tugs towed the *Canadiana* to the Rich Marine dock; the plans for her Cedar Point operation were dead in the water. In 1964, she was again for sale, as other plans for her never came to fruition. Late in 1965 a sale was announced and delayed until July 1966 by an injunction placed upon her for default of payment of docking fees to Rich Marine.

Sam Parella became the *Canadiana's* owner in July 1966 who had her towed back to Cleveland. Parella sold her in March 1967 to Mowbray's Floating Equipment Exchange, who later that month sold her to Waterman Steamship Company - both of New York. Tropicana - the Sarasota, Florida orange juice company - purchased her in 1967 and planned to trade her to the U.S. Maritime

Sitting deep in water up to the Promenade Deck and listing to port at Collision Bend. She is eventually declared a nuisance to navigation and a contract awarded for her removal.

Left: Just before her final trip out of Buffalo, the Canadiana resembles the day she slid down the planks at the Buffalo Dry Dock Company in 1910. Below: The remains of the Canadiana being towed out of Buffalo for the Welland Canal.

Administration for a troopship they wanted to convert into a refrigerated orange juice tanker. Ownership was transferred to Sea-Land Service in 1968, which sold her to Jim Vinci of Cleveland. Vinci was a noted restaurateur with plans to convert the steamer into a restaurant and nightclub with motel style rooms on the third deck. Fire compliance costs made this plan prohibitive.

The *Canadiana* sank at Collision Bend in the Cuyahoga River in Cleveland on February 17, 1982. The power to her pumps had been cut off for failure to pay the electric bills. Declared abandoned, the U.S. Army Corps of Engineers awarded a $256,000 contract to Northrup Contracting to raise her. Eventually refloated, she was towed to Ashtabula, Ohio on June 21, 1983. Purchased by the Friends of the Canadiana, who had plans to restore her and bring her back to operation, they had her towed back to Buffalo on September 17, 1984.

During the summer of 1986, most of her upper deck structure was removed and catalogued, then her hull was towed out of Buffalo, past Crystal Beach to Ramey's Bend in the Welland Canal for hull and engine work. Funding for the project was never secured and her hull was cut up for scrap during the spring of 2004.

Right: Ninety-four years after her launch, American Ship Building Company Hull 215 in the process of being scrapped.

Last Days in Dry Dock

All photos courtesy
Rick Doan
(except as noted)

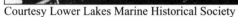

Last Days in Dry Dock

All photos courtesy
Rick Doan
(except as noted)

Courtesy Lower Lakes Marine Historical Society

CHAPTER 5
The 1980s Revival

The virtual monopoly Crystal Beach held on the amusement park trade on the Niagara Frontier for half a century ended in the 1980s. Erie Beach, the closest competitor closed permanently after the summer of 1930. Other amusement centers, such as Fantasy Island (Grand Island), Glen Park (Williamsville), Fun-n-Games Park (Tonawanda), Liberty Park (Cheektowaga), and the Niagara Falls, Ontario parks: Frontier Park, Maple Leaf Village, Marineland, Towerview Park, never developed the draw of local patronage that Crystal Beach enjoyed. That all changed in the early 1980s when Darien Lake became a major amusement park, and Canada's Wonderland near Toronto, Ontario opened. Both offered amusements on the scale that Crystal Beach could not. By the end of the 1982 season, Crystal Beach was in receivership. Buffalo businessman, Ramsi Tick, operated the park for the receivers during 1983 and restored travel to Crystal Beach by boat, albeit only once a week and on a considerably smaller vessel.

Author's collection.

The remains of the Erie Beach pier as it appeared in 2002.

Miss Buffalo II

Miss Buffalo II came from the Gulf of Mexico where she operated as the Marlin Queen, a fishing party vessel with a capacity of 200. Her service to Crystal Beach began on June 30, 1983, and continued every Thursday with three Buffalo departures and three return trips.

New owners took over Crystal Beach in 1984 and negotiated for the return *Miss Buffalo II*. Still operating one day a week, the schedule changed slightly to Friday with two departures from Buffalo at 9:00 AM & 11:00 AM and returning trips at 3:30 PM and 6:30 PM.

For 1985, reportedly, the park searched for another vessel to make weekend excursions from Buffalo to the Park because the *Miss Buffalo II* had already been booked for other business. The *Miss Buffalo II* never returned and three seasons would pass before another vessel brought regular service to the park by a company not affiliated with Crystal Beach.

Miss Buffalo II on Lake Erie.

Courtesy Karl R Josker

This image of the Americana at the Crystal Beach pier was one of the last dockings at Crystal Beach. Black and white reproduction does not do justice to this early evening landing photographed in color on August 27, 1989. This scene was commonplace for nearly three-quarters of a century. Only 29 of Crystal Beach's 100 seasons were without boat service.

Americana

As the 1980s were drawing to a close, Crystal Beach was reportedly doing well after recovering from its financial troubles earlier in the decade. Park owners had successfully reintroduced music and dancing since renovating the dancehall in 1984 and they announced major expansion plans. Reintroducing full-size ferry service to Crystal Beach on a daily basis was an ambitious, financially risky venture. The park's future seemed bright, so, the time may have been right to return regular service to Crystal Beach with a full-size vessel. Ramsi Tick lost his bid to own Crystal Beach but as he had returned boat service to the park in 1983, he wanted to provide service in a manner that mirrored the golden era of the park.

Tick, with business partner Michael Hamann formed the Lake Erie Boat Cruise Corporation and began

Docked in the Buffalo River at the foot of Main Street (just left of the vessel's stern), where most of Americana's predecessors had departed until the Lake Erie Excursion Company opened its own docking facility at the foot of Commercial Street around 1915.

Above: The Americana approaches the Crystal Beach pier. Right: Passengers disembark following Americana's inaugural voyage from Buffalo. The vessel would shortly sport a fresh coat of white paint.

negotiations to purchase the Block Island Ferry in 1987. She arrived in Buffalo on October 15, 1987, and was towed a month later to the Port Weller Dry Docks in Ontario for repairs and renovation. Tick renamed the vessel *Americana*.

Ceremonies at the Buffalo Naval and Servicemen's Park and on the Crystal Beach Pier celebrated her inaugural run on May 21, 1988.

Late in June, just before the busy July 4th holiday, her rudder struck rocks in the Buffalo River near her dock at the Buffalo Naval Park. She had to be towed to Port Colborne for repairs. The new enterprise lost the revenues of a very important holiday.

Around 11:30 PM on August 24, 1988, the Americana struck the rocks again while turning around in the harbor for another run to Crystal Beach to pick up 400 concert goers. The stranded passengers were bussed home. The Lake Erie Boat Cruise Corporation cancelled the balance of the season, because the repairs were going to take longer than the remaining days of the season. The revenues from another holiday weekend were lost.

Lake Erie Boat Cruise Corporation filed for bankruptcy protection in June 1989; hoping revenues from the upcoming season would be enough to pay off its creditors. Tick sited lost revenues from the missed holidays plus the related repairs to the ship's rudder left the company without the income to pay its creditors. The *Americana* resumed service to Crystal Beach late in June 1989.

When Crystal Beach closed forever at the end of the 1989 season, the *Americana* lost its only port of call. The Lake Erie Boat Cruise Corporation managed to keep the vessel running during 1990, offering lake cruises. Ramsi Tick was not successful in generating enough income to pay off creditors and M & T Bank eventually foreclosed on the vessel, and sold it to Caribbean interests in 1991.

Courtesy Karl R Josker

Above: Docked under the Skyway near the Buffalo Naval and Servicemen's Park.

Right: In drydock at Port Weller Dry Docks.

Other Floats of the Parade CHAPTER 6

The following steamers reportedly are connected to Crystal Beach, but their excursions and/or connections to the Crystal Beach Line require confirmation. Also, tug boats came to the assistance of Crystal Beach Line steamers and those that had to sail to Crystal Beach to do so are duly presented.

Rochester - A steamer of Canadian registry, she came from Montreal, Quebec in 1863 and built by A. Cantin. She had numerous owners, far to many to be listed here (15 different owners between 1863 and 1869 alone). Rebuilt four different times, the *Rochester* sailed under three other names: *Hastings* (1876), *Eurydice* (1890), and *Donnelly* (1899). She spent her entire existence on Lake Ontario, except for 1898 when she sailed between Buffalo and Crystal Beach. Further research may turn up confirmation of her 1898 commission.

Empire - At the onset of the 1906 season, John Rebstock announced that the steamer *Empire* would work the Crystal Beach Line along with the *State of New York*. According to Rebstock, *Empire* was built in Montreal in 1905, but she is a bit of a mystery ship as there are no records in U.S. or Canadian registries that match Rebstock's description. It is possible he may have been referring to the steamer *Empire State*, but she was built by Bidwell & Mason in 1862, and there is no record of her sailing to Crystal Beach.

Top: Rochester as Eurydice - as she may have sailed to Crystal Beach. Above: The Empire State - may have been Rebstock's Empire, but there is no history of her sailing to Crystal Beach.

Owana - Once the *Pennsylvania,* the *Owana* was under negotiations for a commission on the Crystal Beach Line. It is reasonable to assume that negotiations fell apart based on a lack of evidence that she ever sailed to Crystal Beach.

Champion - Built by George T. Davie in 1877 at Levis, Quebec and first used as a towboat. She had a number of owners including the Canadian Pacific Railway, and her name changed in 1888 to *Cambria*. She struck log raft, which had broken away from a tug during gale on July 28, 1897 near Point Edward, Ontario, Lake Huron, damaging her engine. The vessel was sold 1902 for use between Buffalo and Crystal Beach. On her way to the new owners and her Crystal Beach Line commission, *Cambria's* crew abandoned her at Martindale Pond in the Welland Canal, St. Catherines but the reason was not disclosed. Eventually, the steamer found her way to Allenburg, Ontario and dismantled in 1905. Although *Champion*, as *Cambria,* never sailed between Buffalo and Crystal Beach, she could be considered one of the Crystal Beach Line fleet if confirmation of this purchase can be confirmed.

Garnet - Rebstock divulged even less about the steamer *Garnet* than the Rochester when he announced the steamer would join the Crystal Beach Line in 1906. He noted only that the steamer was a wood hulled vessel and built on the St. Lawrence in 1903. Like the *Empire*, there is no apparent record of the *Garnet* apart from the photo at left. Confirmation of her sailing to Crystal Beach either as a vessel of the Line or a charter remain to be found.

Top: The Owana negotiated for a Crystal Beach Line Commission. Center: Champion as the Cambria - intended for Crystal Beach but never made it. Bottom: The Garnet at an unidentified location.

Vision - Crystal Beach Park sponsored the Buffalo Yacht Club's annual regatta in 1893, and the steamer *Vision* sailed from Buffalo to Crystal Beach for use by the regatta judges and for spectators willing to pay a premium to observe the regatta from her decks. Details of *Vision's* history are not in the general archives of Great Lakes marine records. However, articles in Buffalo newspapers indicate Sloan & Cowles owned and operated *Vision* between Buffalo and the area resorts from 1890 through the summer of 1894.

Myrtle - A little commuter, *Myrtle,* transported her passengers from the Crystal Beach pier to points west along the Point Abino Bay shore starting in 1899. Web Haun operated the commuter.

Marion L - Another little commuter built in Ridgeway, Ontario in 1912, providing service on the same route as the *Myrtle*.

Adralexa - Reportedly a "small yacht" to run between the Crystal Beach pier and Point Abino in 1900. Whether the *Adralexa* is the *Myrtle* or the *Marion L* renamed, or a different vessel is unknown as the *Adralexa* is not documented in any manner.

Top: The Myrtle commuting on the waters of Point Abino Bay. Center: The Myrtle in dry dock - probably near the Buffalo Yacht Club on Point Abino. Right: Marion L docked at the Crystal Beach pier. Her home port of St. Catharines is stenciled on her bow under her name.

Myrtle photos courtesy of the Lower Lakes Marine Historical Society and Harvey Holzworth.

Courtesy of the Niagara Falls Public Library, Niagara Falls, Ontario.

Tugs to the Rescue

Grace Danforth - Built in Buffalo by the Union Dry Dock Company in 1888. She towed the *Gazelle* to Crystal Beach after a midlake breakdown on August 9, 1898. The tug foundered on Lake Erie during a voyage from Cleveland, Ohio to Buffalo on December 21, 1921. Eight lives were lost.

Cascade - The *White Star* broke down on June 4, 1906. The *Cascade* not only came to her rescue, she towed the *White Star* back to Crystal Beach later that evening so she could bring back at least some of the passengers from earlier that day. The Union Dry Dock Company in Buffalo also built *Cascade* in 1895. She was dismantled during 1916.

Alpha - Built in Chicago by the Chicago Dredge & Dock Company in 1881, she came to Buffalo in 1901 when the Hand & Johnson Tug Line (Great Lakes Towing Co.) purchased her. *Alpha* assisted the *Cascade* with the disabled *White Star*. Her fifth owner, Andrew J. Harper, abandoned the tug in Baltimore, Maryland. By that time, she had also been renamed *Kentucky*.

Glenora - On August 24, 1900, the *Gazelle's* "shoe" struck a rock near the Crystal Beach pier. Unable to proceed on her own, the *Glenora* towed the *Gazelle* back to Buffalo.

From top to bottom: Grace Danforth, Cascade, Alpha.

A Note on Preservation

CHAPTER 7

Images courtesy of Harvey Holzworth except as noted.

The S.S. Canadiana Preservation Society, Inc. (CPSI) saved the Canadiana's engine from the cutter's torch and smelter. Harvey Hozworth, president of CPSI hopes that the group will be able to restore the engine to an operating display for the new Buffalo State College Maritime Museum, proposed for a site near the Peace Bridge not far from the Frank Lloyd Wright boathouse. The 65-ton engine was moved in April 2006 from Sandrin Dry Dock, near Port Colborne to Buffalo. Moved in the early morning hours, the Peace Bridge was closed to traffic until the engine, loaded on a flat bed, was safely across.

CPSI was instrumental in saving the pilothouse from rot by having it moved to the Buffalo State College boat shop at the Port of Buffalo off Fuhrmann Boulevard in preparation for its refurbishment as both a learning tool and historical artifact.

The restored pilothouse and other remnants of the Canadiana are destined for the proposed Buffalo State College Maritime Museum.

Canadiana's triple expansion engine waits transporting to Buffalo.

Courtesy of the Niagara Falls Public Library, Niagara Falls, Ontario

Top left: Tipped on its side, the triple expansion engine loaded on a flatbed truck waiting for its trip back to Buffalo - the wheels of the flatbed add perspective to the size of the engine.

Above: The pilothouse being lowered from the boat deck before the Canadiana was towed to the Welland Canal during earlier restoration efforts.

Left: The Canadiana departs Crystal Beach circa 1920.

Appendix

Photo: Karl R. Josker.

Americana heading toward the setting sun and Crystal Beach.

Appendix TABLE 1: ANNUAL COMPOSITION OF THE CRYSTAL BEACH LINE

Expanded from a table by Jack Messmer, Lower Lakes Marine Historical Society.

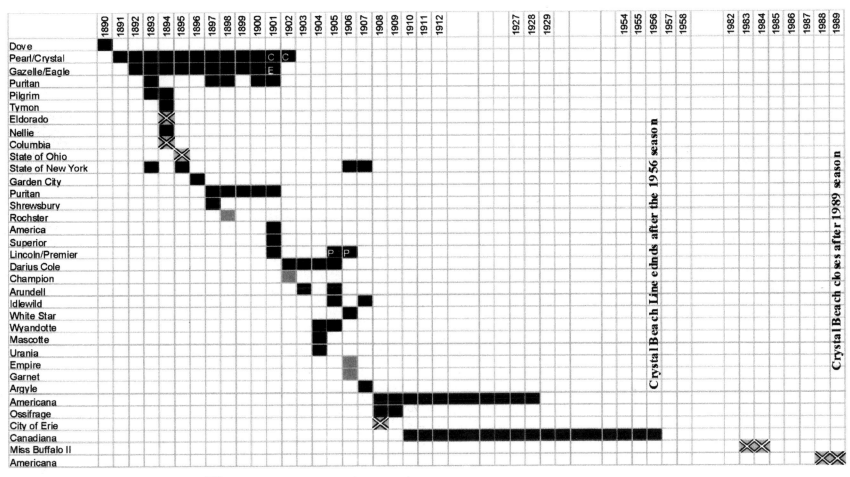

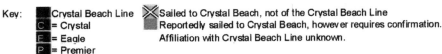

Key:
- ■ Crystal Beach Line
- C = Crystal
- E = Eagle
- P = Premier
- ✕ Sailed to Crystal Beach, not of the Crystal Beach Line
- ▨ Reportedly sailed to Crystal Beach, however requires confirmation.
- Affiliation with Crystal Beach Line unknown.

Appendix
TABLE 2: ROUTE OF THE MESECK LINE STEAMERS

Author's collection.

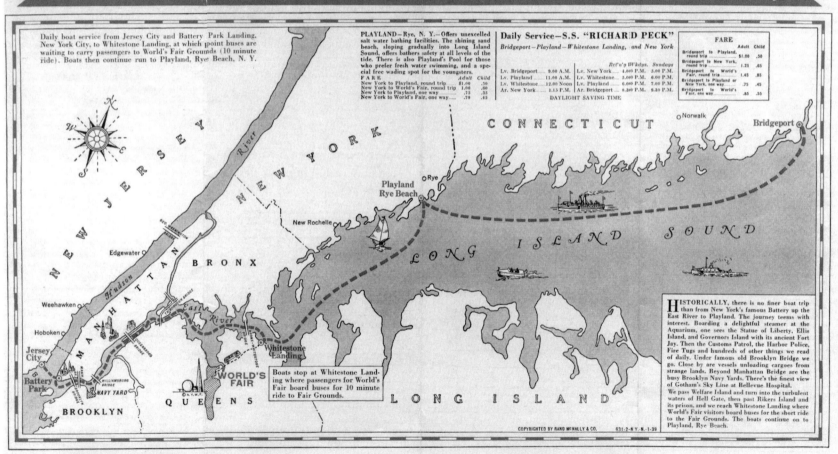

Appendix TABLE 3: VESSEL STATISTICS BY LENGTH

Vessel	Type	Length	Width	Depth	Hull	Disposition
City of Erie	Paddle	316.0	44.0	14.0	Steel	Ceased all operations in 1938. Towed to the Otis Steel Company in Cleveland in 1941 and scrapped.^
State of Ohio	Paddle	225.2	32.4	13.3	Iron	Burned at Cleveland, May 20, 1924. Converted to a barge. Stranded on Lorrain, Ohio breakwall, December 17, 1929 - total loss.
Americana	Screw	209.7	45.0	15.8	Steel	Scrapped in Baltimore, Maryland, October 1953.
Canadiana	Screw	209.7	45.0	15.8	Steel	Sank 1982. Raised 1983 and towed to Buffalo for restoration. Hull scrapped in 2004.
State of New York	Paddle	203.0	32.3	10.4	Iron	Dismantled, 1936. Rebuilt as barge, suffered a fire and sank, 1954
Darius Cole	Paddle	201.3	32.4	9.3	Iron	Burned off Barcelona, NY, on September 1, 1925,
Dove	Paddle	187.8	24.3	8.4	Wood	Burned at Toledo on November 24, 1897.
Argyle	Paddle	185.0	26.0	9.6	Wood	Sank in Chatham, Ontario, 1918. scrapped in 1920.
Garden City	Screw	177.9	26.1	10.0	Steel	Unknown. Drops from Canadian List of Shipping after 1945
Pearl Crystal	Paddle	177.0	28.7	10.0	Wood	Sank in Niagara River in 1904. Scrapped During or shortly after December 1905.
Urania	Paddle	174.3	27.7	10.6	Wood	Burned on December 2, 1912 while being dismantled.
White Star	Paddle	167.2	25.3	8.2	Wood	Burned on March 1, 1926 at Hamilton, Ontario. Converted to a barge. Abandoned in 1940. Remains salvaged in 1949 and converted to a sand sucker. Reported that the iron hull became a breakwater at Kingston during 1975.**
America	Screw	164.6	31.0	11.0	Steel	Struck a reef and beached off Isle Royale on June 7, 1928, and sank during salvage efforts.
Ossifrage	Screw	161.6	27.8	9.0	Wood	Foundered in Northumberland Straits on September 25, 1919.

Vessel	Type	Length	Width	Depth	Hull	Disposition
Shrewsbury	Paddle	161.5	26.5	7.3	Wood	Reported abandoned in 1911.
Idlewild	Paddle	160.9	26.0	7.4	Iron	Dismantled in 1914, registered as a barge in 1919.. Assumed destroyed in Peekskill after 1923.
Wyandotte	Screw	155.6	35.0	9.0	Steel	Scrapped in 1940
Puritan	Screw	145.0	32.0	Unknown	Unknown	Last registered as a barge in 1936
Rochester	Paddle	142.0	24.0	Unknown	Wood	Abandoned 1914.
Puritan	Twin Screw	138.7	32.0	9.8	Wood	Burned on July 14, 1901. Rebuilt as a tug, burned again on January 6, 1906 then converted to a barge. last registered in Canada in 1936.
Arundell	Paddle	136.5	23.3	11.0	Iron	Sunk in collision with Lake Stirling, on James River, North Carolina, on April 21, 1922
Mascotte	Screw	133.6	30.0	8.6	Steel	Partially burned in winter quarters, January 28, 1934 in the Chicago River. Final enrollment surrendered at Chicago, January 28, 1939. U.S. Corps of Engineers advertised for bids to remove wreck in June, 1948.
Champion	Paddle	131.2	23.3	10.6	Wood	Dismantled June 1905.
Lincoln Premier	Screw	130.0	25.2	9.0	Wood	Burned, then sank. Bruce Mines, Ontario. November 13, 1920
Gazelle Eagle	Screw	123.0	25.0	9.5	Wood	Abandoned in Chicago River and burned by Us. Gov't. Dec. 21, 1908
Pilgrim	Screw	113.7	26.0	7.9	Unknown	Destroyed by fire in Bayonne, New Jersey on March 27, 1937.
A. J. Tyron	Screw	112.4	21.9	7.4	Wood	Burned as a spectacle suitable for the celebration of civic holiday on August 2, 1929.*
Columbia	Screw	109.0	20.0	9.0	Wood	Burned and sank during October of 1917.
Nellie	Screw	104.5	25.8	7.4	Wood	Burned to water's edge on May 18, 1903 in Detroit.
Superior	Screw	98.0	29.9	10.0	Wood	Converted into a tug, circa 1918. Burned on May 6, 1920.
Eldorado	Screw	73.3	17.0	6.3	Unknown	Burned December 16, 1908 at Phippsburg, Maine.

*Scanner, Monthly News Bulletin of the Toronto Marine Historical Society. v. 5, n. 7 (April 1973)
**Scanner, Monthly News Bulletin of the Toronto Marine Historical Society. v. 8, n. 2 (November 1975)
^Anchor News, March/April 1983.

Appendix

TABLE 4: S. S. CANADIANA OWNERS AND MASTERS

LAKE ERIE EXCURSION COMPANY

George S. Riley	1910 - 1917
John Mitchell	1916, 1917
J. H. Grant	1917

BUFFALO & CRYSTAL BEACH CORP.

Alfred Johnson	1919 - 1931
Austin Wilcock	1926, 1928, 1929

CRYSTAL BEACH TRANSIT CO.

Austin Wilcock	1934 - 1937
William Brooks	1938, 1939
William F. Malloy	1940 - 1956
Edward Solmonson	1953, 1954, 1956

SEAWAY EXCURSION LINES

Philip E. Thrope	May 22, 1958

LUCAS COUNT BANK

TOLEDO EXCURSION LINES

Joseph Wiepert	January 5, 1959

PLEASURAMA EXCURSION LINES

H. S. Harding	December 5, 1960

SAM PERELLA
MOBARYS FLOATING EQP. EXCHANGE, INC.
WATERMAN STEAMSHIP CORP.
TROPICANA PRODUCTS, INC.
SEA-LAND SERVICE, INC.
MARITIME ADMINISTRATION
JIM VINCI
NORTHRUP CONTRACTING CO.
FRIENDS OF THE CANADIANA
CANADIANA RESTORATION PROJECT

Appendix TABLE 5: STEAMER DATA BY YEAR BUILT

Steamer	Capacity	Builder	Year Built	Steamer	Capacity	Builder	Year Built
Dove	-	Alvin A. Turner, Detroit	1867	Shrewsburry	850	Bath Iron Works	1887
Gazelle/Eagle	850	George Irwin, Detroit	1873	Lincoln/Premier	800-850	Simpson, Melancthon	1888
Pearl/Crystal	1300	John Pepper Clark, Detroit	1875	Superior	1200	Cleveland Dry Dock Co.	1890
Urania	800	Wolf & Davidson	1875	Pilgrim	800	David Bell	1891
Arundell	-	David Bell, Buffalo.	1876	Columbia	1000	W. Murphy	1892
Idlewild	1200	Detroit Dry Dock Company	1879	Garden City	1200	John Doty Engine Works	1892
Argyle	-	Jamieson	1879	Wyandotte	-	Detroit Dry Dock Company	1892
State of Ohio	-	Detroit Dry Dock Company	1880	Puritan	1500	Robert Mills & Company	1893
Nellie	-	Michael Laprise	1882	Eldorado	250	Sloan & Cowles	1893
State of New York	-	Detroit Dry Dock Company	1883	White Star	-	W. C. White	1897
Tymon	700	David Foster	1884	City of Erie	-	Detroit Dry Dock Company	1898
Darius Cole	1800	Globe Ship Building Co.	1885	Americana	3500	American Ship Building Co. at the Buffalo Dry Dock Co.	1908
Mascotte	-	Detroit Dry Dock Company	1885				
Ossifrage	-	F. W. Wheeler & Company	1886	Canadiania	3500	American Ship Building Co. at the Buffalo Dry Dock Co.	1910

Compiled from News Paper Articles, Bowling Green State University Historical Collections of the Great Lakes vessel files, Great Lakes Marine Collection of the Milwaukee Public Library, newspaper articles.

Appendix TABLE 6: KNOWN CREW OF THE CRYSTAL BEACH LINE

AMERICANA

George S. Riley (c)	1908, 1909
William Lucas (f)	1908, 1909
William Lucas (c)	1926
William Stern (ce)	1908, 1909
Cornelius Ames (p)	1908
F.S. Paddock (ce)	1912
Robert Bailey (d)	1913
Jack Frankenberg (d)	1913
Frank Dimond (d)	1913
Fred Macy (w)	1913
1st Mate Brooks (f)	1913
Purser Paull (p)	1913
Thomas Ryan (wl)	1913
Alfred H. Johnson (c)	1911-1916, 1918-1919, 1929
John McLeod (c)	1918-1921, 1924
John Gooldorf (ce)	1918, 1919
Ed Smith (ce)	1921, 1924 1926, 1928
Austin Wilcock (c)	1927, 1928

CANADIANA

Captains: See Appendix Table 4	
William Stern (ce)	1910
William Lucas (f)	1910
Edward Carmicheal (p)	1910
Tom Riley (ce)	1912
J.C. Stewart (f)	1918
Frank Caddock (f)	1918
Frank Paddock* (ce)	1919-1921, 1926, 1928, 1935
Marvin White (fr)	1920s
Jerry Kelleher (d)	1930s
Fred Larson (wl)	1935
James Hanratty (fr)	1937
James Linton (ce)	1937-1941
Arthur J. Madigan (s)	1940
William C. Rohe (e)	1942
Thomas Fagen (f)	1943
Frank Dimond (w)	1943
William Warner (ce)	1942-1950
George Hans (ce)	1951-1956

CANADIANA (cont'd.)

Don MacPhearson (se)	1951
Ralph E. Greene (f)	1956
Herb Hewitt (p)	194?-195?
Ed Hettich (ap)	?
Charles W. Michaels (d)	?

ARUNDELL

Byron Armstrong (c)	1905

CITY OF ERIE

Hugh McAlpine (c)	1908
Edward S. Pickell (c)	1908

CRYSTAL

Captain Campau (c)	1902

DARIUS COLE

W. E. Comer (c)	1902
Captain Phillips (c)	1903
John J. Cassin (c)	1904, 1905
J.R. Blanchette (ce)	1904
C.L. Barron (ce)	1905
George S. Riley (f)	?

EAGLE

John R. Glover (c)	1901
Thomas Newman (c)	1901

IDLEWILD

John C. Doran (ce)	1905

GARDEN CITY

Captain Cooney (c)	1896

GAZELLE

Thomas Doyle (c)	1892
George Swift (c)	1894, 1897
Captain McRea (c)	1897
Thomas Dancy (f)	1898
Captain Campau (c)	1898, 1900
Captain Hewitt (c)	1900

OSSIFRAGE

J.T. Stockwell (c)	1909
George Caister (ce)	1901

PEARL

Daniel Coughlin (c)	1891
John Edwards (c)	1892
William C. Burnett (c)	1893
Captain McLarty (c)	1893, 1894
William Dent (fa)	1893
J.H. Jones (d)	1893
Alex Walters (c)	1896-1898
Thomas Dancy (f)	1898

PREMIER

J. T. Stockwell (c)	1907
Oscar Pierce (p)	1907

PURITAN

Abner Gilbert (c)	1893
John O'Brien (c)	1897
Captain Pearsons (c)	1901
James Fontaine (c)	?

SHREWSBURY

James Fontaine (c)	1897

STATE OF NEW YORK

U. S. Cody (f)	1893, 1895
John J. Cassin (c)	1906
George S. Riley (c)	1907
James Middleton (ce)	1907

A. J. TYMON

James McSherry (c)	1894

SUPERIOR

Captain Hewitt: (c)	1891
John R. Glover (c)	1891

WHITE STAR

Captain Parkington (c)	1906
George S. Riley (c)	1906

ap = assistant purser
c = captain
ce = chief engineer
d = deckhand
e = engineer
f = first mate
fa = first assistant
fr = fireman
wl = wheelsman
p = purser
s = seaman
se = second engineer
w = watchman
? = citation does not specidy year(s) served.

———————————

Year(s) noted for service were noted in the citation and does not imply that the individuals served only during the year(s) indicated.

———————————

Sources:
Historical Collections of the Great Lakes, Bowling Green State University, Great Lakes Maritime Personnel Online Database. http://www.bgsu.edu/colleges/library/hcgl/ppldb.html

Great Lakes Red Books

Buffalo news papers

S.S. Canadiana History Book (Unpublished manuscript) by Floyd Baker

*In the Great Lakes Red Books, there are listings for H.S. Paddock, F.S. Paddock, F.J. Paddock holding the poisitions of chief engineer. It is assumed that all of these are Frank Paddock. It is possible that Frank Paddock is also the first officer Frank Caddock.

Appendix
TABLE 7: VESSLES & OFFICIAL NUMBERS
HARVARD TRAINER SPECIFICATIONS

Vessel	Official No.	Vessel	Official No.
Alpha	106036	Idlewild	85595
America	107367	Lewiston	116110
Americana	205096	Lincoln	92735
Americana/Block Is.	226004	Mascotte	91772
Argyle	72998	Nellie	130224
Arundell	105784	Ossifrage	155124
Avon	105733	Pearl/Crystal	150032
Bapst, Frank L.	120993	Pilgrim	150524
Canadiania	207479	Premier	92735
Cascade	127088	Puritan	150630
Champion	74297	Rochester	94988
City of Erie	127242	Shrewsbury	116152
Columbia	126872	State of New York	126150
Conestoga	125669	State of Ohio	125808
Darius Cole	157173	Superior	116357
Dove	6512	Tashmoo	145843
Eldorado	136349	Tymon	73920
Garden City	100035	Urania	120210
Gazelle/Eagle	85272	White Star	103961
Grace Danforth	86017	Wyandotte	81406

HARVARD TRAINER SPECIFICATIONS

Engine:	Pratt & Whitney R-1340-AN-1 Wasp, 600 hp, radial
Wingspan:	42 feet 0.5 inches (12.8 m)
Length:	28 feet 11 inches (8.8 m)
Height:	11 feet 9 inches (3.5 m)
Weight (empty):	3,995 pounds (1,812 kg)
Weight (gross):	5,235 pounds (2375 kg)
Cruising speed:	140 miles per hour (225 km/h)
Maximum speed:	180 miles per hour (290 km/h)
Rate of Climb:	1,300 feet per minute (396 m/min.)
Service ceiling:	22,000 feet (6,710 m)
Range:	710 miles (1,143 km)

Source: Harvard Historical Aviation Centre, Springbrook, Alberta, http://www.penholdbase.com/

If the nose of the Harvard Trainer struck the water 75 feet away from the Canadiana, then its wingtip was only 54 feet from the ship.

Some local divers claim to have found some of the wreckage but remain secretive about its exact location.

Appendix IMAGES

Captain George S. Riley
Americana & Canadiana
1908

Captain James P. Fontaine
Shrewsbury
Buffalo Evening News
June 10, 1943

Captain Alfred H. Johnson
Americana & Canadiana
Buffalo Courier Express
July 6, 1930

Captain John J. Cassin
State of New York
Buffalo Courier Express
August 5, 1906

Frank Kirby
Naval Architect*
Alan Hall Collection.

Ramsi Tick
Restored limited boat
service to Crystal Beach
in 1983 a quarter century
after the Crystal Beach
Line ceased operations.
May 18, 1988

*Kirby was 59 years old when the Americana was launched in 1908.

Captain William Malloy
Canadiana
Circa 1954

Captain Austin Wilcock
Americana & Canadiana
Buffalo Courier Express
July 19, 1936

Captain William Brooks
Canadiana
Buffalo Evening News
May 22, 1938

Chief Engineer James Linton
Canadiana
Buffalo, Evening News
July 30, 1942

Captains Malloy and Wilcock (left) appear to be ogling the bathing beauties on the upper deck of the Crystal Beach pier watching the Canadiana dock in this image photographed in 1952. At the time, Malloy was the Canadiana's captain and probably in the pilot house. Buffalo Courier Express, August 10, 1952.

Appendix IMAGES

Library of Congress, Prints and Photographs Division [Reproduction Number LC-USZ62-126578 DLC].

Library of Congress, Prints and Photographs Division [Reproduction Number LC-USZ62-126148 DLC].

Top: The Americana idling up to the dock in 1911. Above: From 1909, the steamer Western States of the D & C Line blocks most of the Main Street dock facilities while the Americana hangs back waiting for space to open up.

Courtesy of Cathy Herbert

Above left: The Idlehour was not a steamer of the Crystal Beach Line, but did have a minor collision with one of its steamers.

Above: Inside the cabin of the Hurricane Deck.

Left: The at-grade railroad crossings at the Main Street dock. The danger of passing trains was always a concern.

Appendix IMAGES

Courtesy of Cathy Herbert

Top: Another faded image of the Gazelle docked at Crystal Beach in 1894.

Above: Ad for the Riverside Businessmen's Association Day at Crystal Beach. Riverside Review, August 6, 1953

Right: Fueling up.

Courtesy of Cathy Herbert

No. 29

The Crystal Beach

Steamboat and Ferry

Company.

BOND.

Courtesy of Cathy Herbert

Courtesy of Harvey Holzworth

Courtesy of Harvey Holzworth

Left: Front cover of CBSFC Mortgage Bond. Top: On guard on the Canadiana's Hurricane Deck. Above: A lifeboat drill on the Canadiana.

Courtesy of Harvey Holzworth

Top: The Marion L at one of her Point Abino Bay stops, the Buffalo Canoe Club. Inset left: A life preserver from the Marion L. Insert right: Harvey Holzworth holding the prized life preserver, July 2007.

1940

2005

Courtesy of Cathy Herbert

Author's collection

Americana Orlop Deck

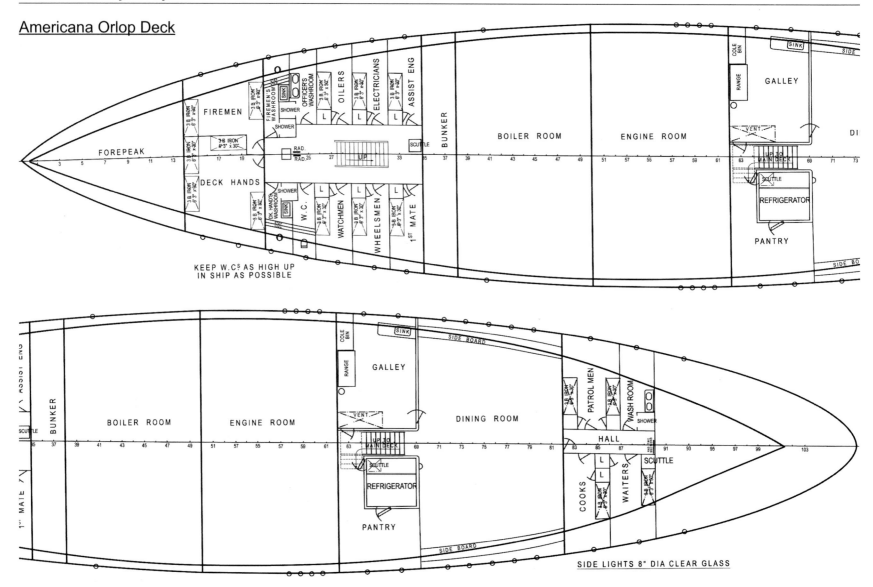

Prints courtesy of Historical Collections of the Great Lakes, Bowling Green State University.

Canadiana Orlop Deck

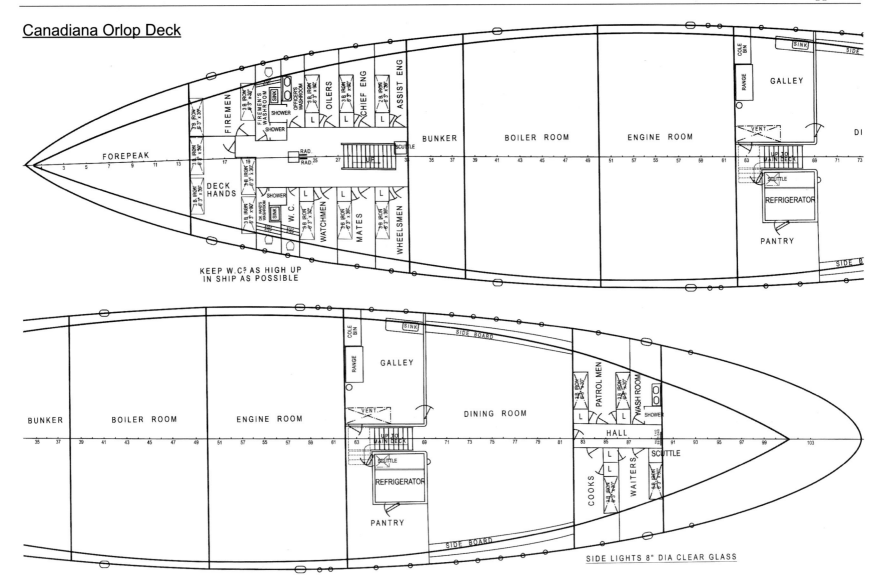

Some of the differences between the Orlop Decks of the Americana and the Canadiana are very subtle, such as the Canadiana's slightly larger coal bunker.

Americana Main Deck

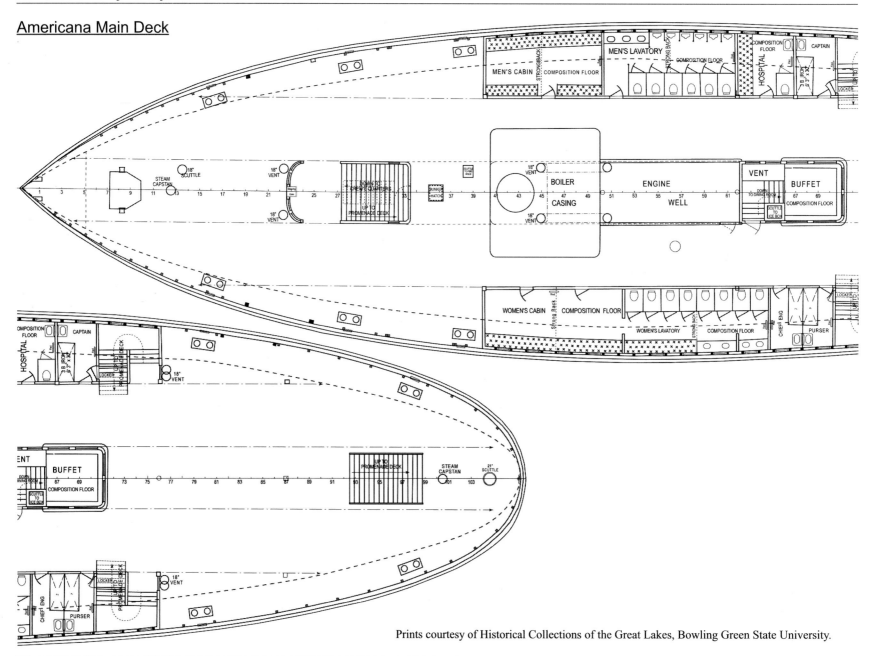

Prints courtesy of Historical Collections of the Great Lakes, Bowling Green State University.

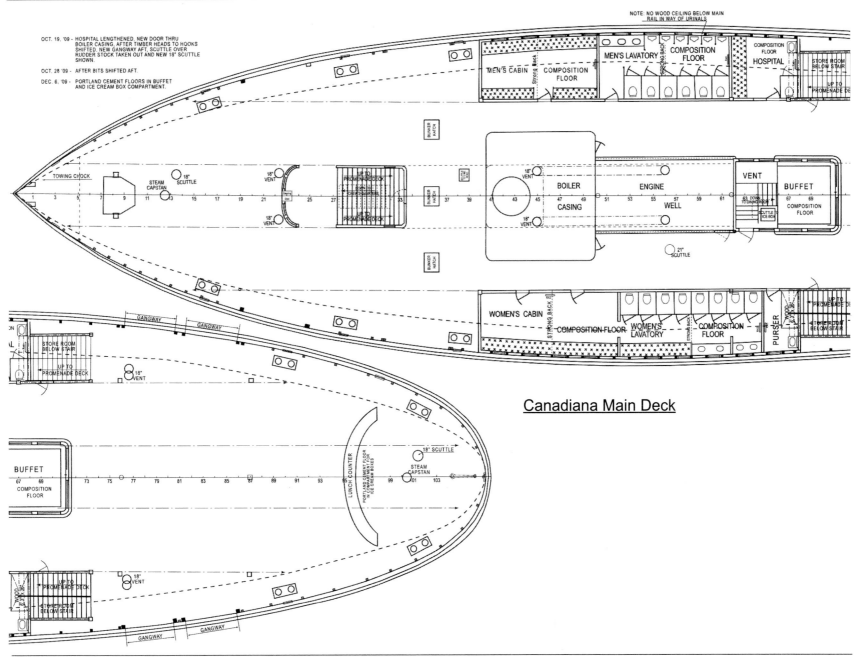

OCT. 19, '09 - HOSPITAL LENGTHENED. NEW DOOR THRU
BOILER CASING. AFTER TIMBER HEADS TO HOOKS
SHIFTED. NEW GANGWAY AFT, SCUTTLE OVER
RUDDER STOCK TAKEN OUT AND NEW 18" SCUTTLE
SHOWN.

OCT. 28 '09 - AFTER BITS SHIFTED AFT.

DEC. 6, '09 - PORTLAND CEMENT FLOORS IN BUFFET
AND ICE CREAM BOX COMPARTMENT.

Canadiana Main Deck

Americana Promenade Deck

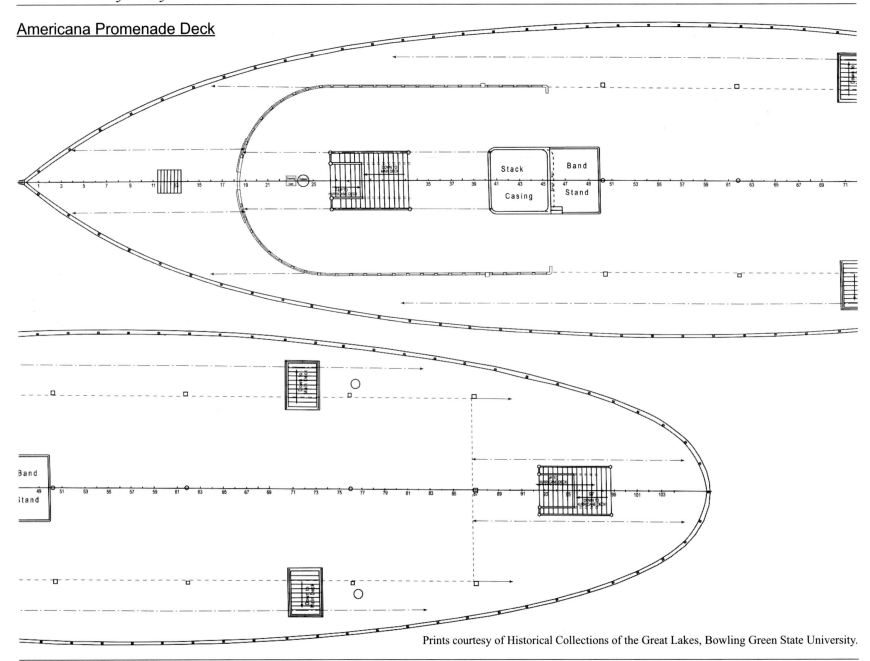

Prints courtesy of Historical Collections of the Great Lakes, Bowling Green State University.

Canadiana Promenade Deck

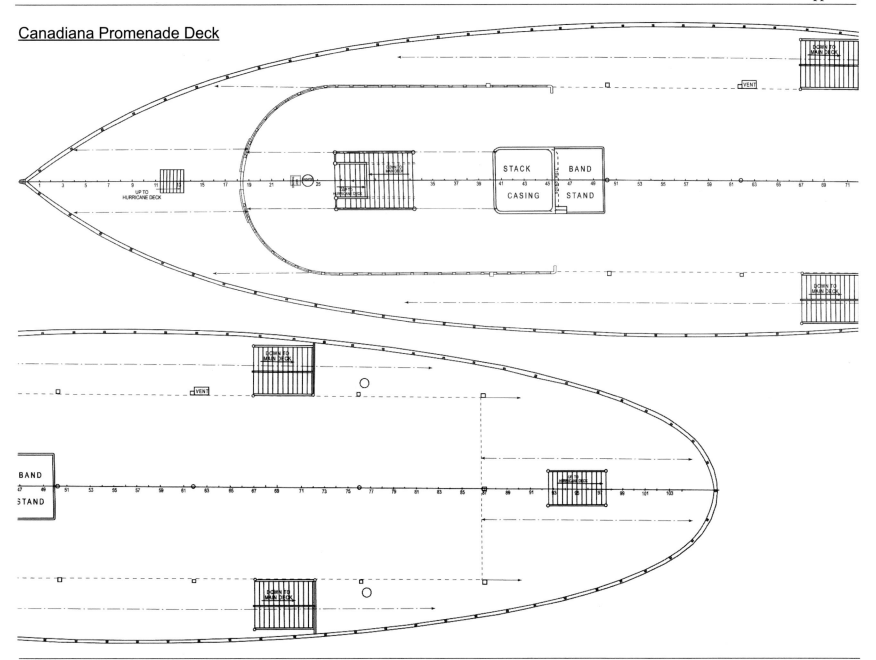

Americana Hurricane Deck

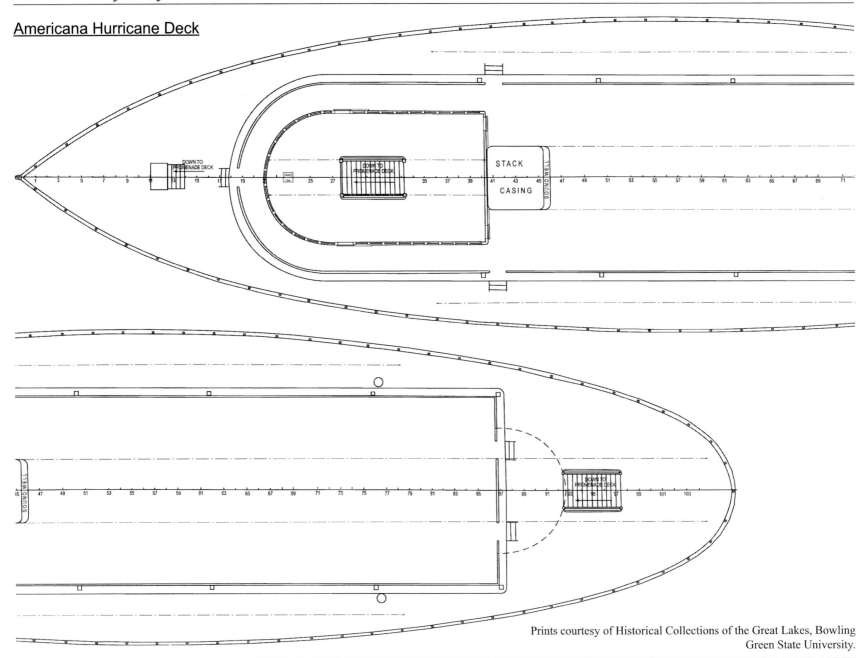

Prints courtesy of Historical Collections of the Great Lakes, Bowling Green State University.

Canadiana Hurricane Deck

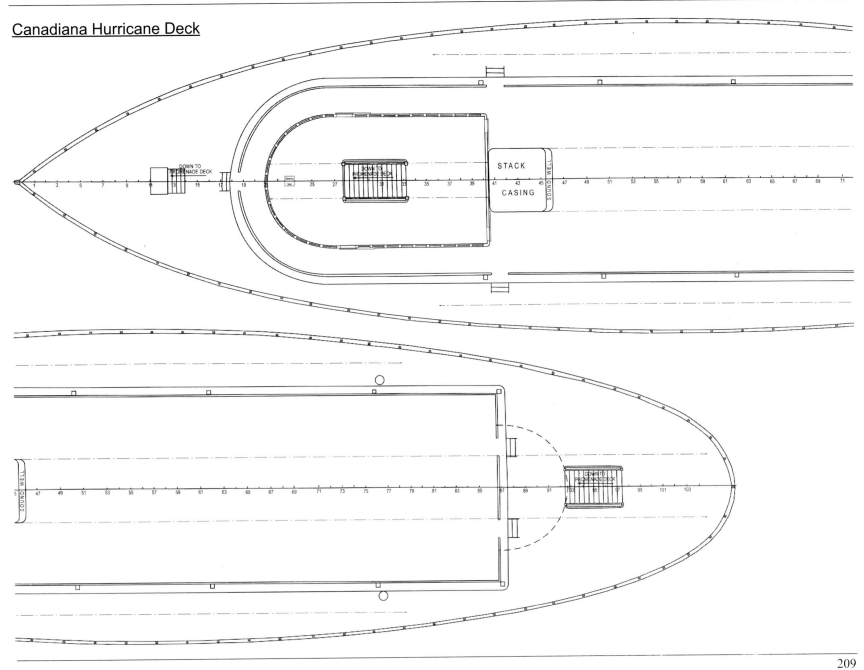

Americana Boat Deck

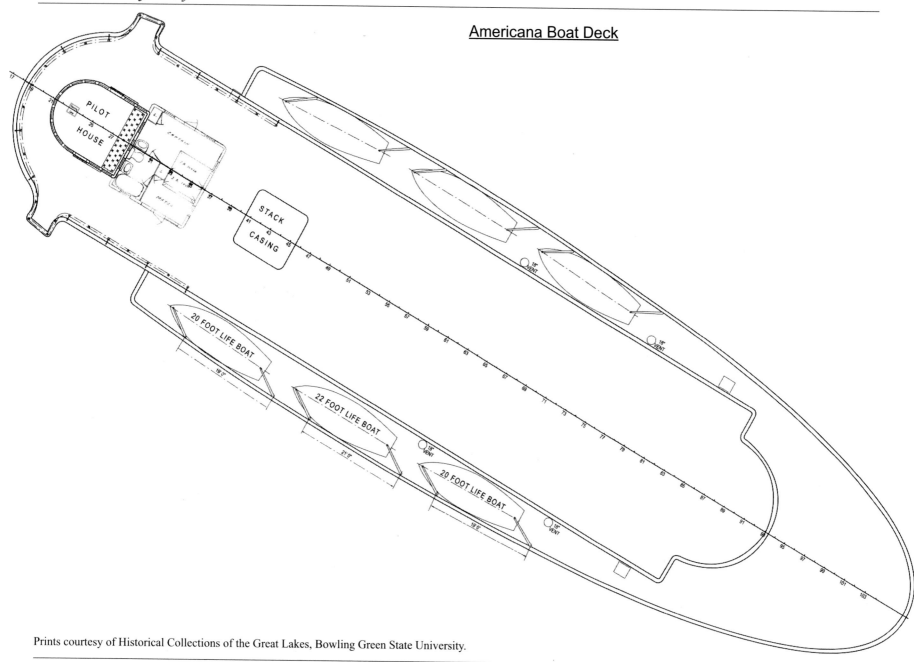

PILOT HOUSE

STACK CASING

20 FOOT LIFE BOAT

22 FOOT LIFE BOAT

20 FOOT LIFE BOAT

Prints courtesy of Historical Collections of the Great Lakes, Bowling Green State University.

Canadiana Boat Deck

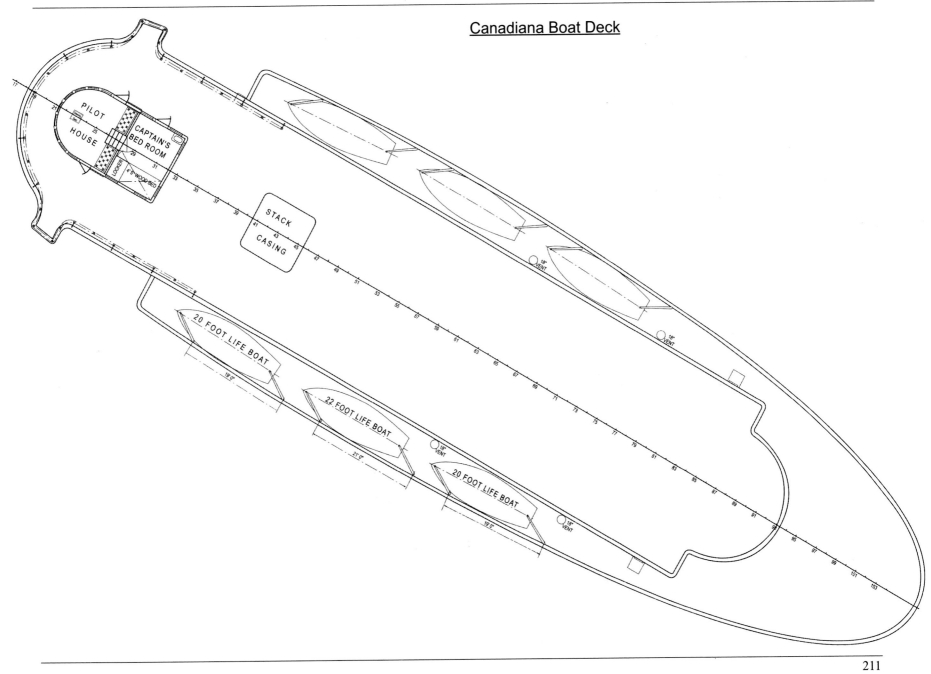

Bibliography

Vessel Files:

Statistics and historical information for most of the vessels are contained in the files of the following collections:

Bowling Green State University, The Historical Collections of the Great Lakes.

Milwaukee Public Library, The Great Lakes Marine Collection

Official Numbers found in the Appendix, Table 7.

Newspapers and other sources sited as follows complete the vessel profiles.

CHAPTER 2:

The Early Steamers:

Zillmer, A.T. "The Lake erie Excursion Company." Inland Seas, Vol. 16, No.4, 1960

"Crystal Beach's Opening." Buffalo Express, May 24, 1901.

"Crystal Beach Rights to be Sold to the Detroit and Buffalo Line." Buffalo Express, November 1, 1906.

(Inland Seas courtesy of the Lower Lakes Marine Historical Society, Buffalo, New York.)

Dove:

"A New Summer resort. Crystal Beach Near Poit Abino to be Made Popular." Buffalo Courier, July 13, 1890.

Marine Review, October 5, 1899 11-3. (From the report of her fire in 1891, until the time she was destoryed 8 years later, she is reported to have had three different owners, Captain Ira Holt - owner at the time of the blaze; Captain Cole - owner one month later; Captain George Daily.)

"The Steamer Dove Burned." Buffalo Enquirer, Wednesday, June 24, 1891.

Marine Review, July 16, 1891.

Port Huron Daily Times, Saturday, June 3, 1899.

U.S. Supreme Court. THE DOVE, 91 U.S. 381 (1875).

Marine Review and Port Huron Daily Times from the Maritime History of the Great Lakes, Walter Lewis. http://www.hhpl.on.ca/GreatLakes/HomePort.asp

Pearl:

"Buffalo Yacht Club's Annual at Crystal Beach." Buffalo Express, August 13, 1893

"No Helping Hand. Deckhand Roberts of the Pearl Falls Overboard." Buffalo Express, August 13, 1893.

"The Victim of Indifference." Buffalo Evening News, August 16, 1893.

P.H. Walter. The Marine Record, June 23, 1887.

"Amusement Park a Religious Assembly Ground." The times Review, Fort Erie, Ontario. November 16,1977.

"Steamer Pearl Ashore?" New York Times, July 8, 1980

"Pearl Aground." Buffalo Express, July 8, 1900.

"Pearl was Saved." Buffalo Express, July 9, 1900.

Cleveland Herald. September 14, 1878.

Cleveland Herald. September 16, 1878.

Chicago Inter Ocean. September 19, 1878.

"Flames on Steamer Pearl." Buffalo Express, July 15, 1900.

Marine Record, Cleveland Herald and the Chicago Inter Ocean from the Maritime History of the Great Lakes, Walter Lewis. http://www.hhpl.on.ca/GreatLakes/HomePort.asp

Images on the previous page, clockwise from upper left corner: City of Erie post card, Arundell as Jasmine, Puritan, State of Ohio, Americana(1988), Canadiana, Crystal Beach pier with wood deck walkway, postcard of Americana's stern and the foot of Main Street, State of New York post card. Center: Crystal Beach ad with the Pearl in the foreground. Postcards from the author's collection.

Crystal:
"Crystal Beach's Opening." Buffalo Express, May 24, 1901.

"Boat was Crowded." Buffalo Express, May 31, 1902.

"News of the Lakes. Passenger Steamer Crystal got a Log in her Wheel Yesterday." Buffalo Express, July 8, 1902.

"Crystal Breaks Down." Buffalo Express, September 1, 1902.

"Crystal Beach Boats." Buffalo Express, April 26, 1903.

Buffalo Evcning News, October 6, 1904..

Buffalo Morning Express, April 14, 1905.

"Wrecked Steamer Crystal to be Removed." Buffalo Evening News, May 26, 1905.

"Excursion Steamer Crystal Released." Buffalo Evening News, December 18, 1905

Auction
"At Crystal Beach, International Assembly on the Chautauqua Plan." Buffalo Courier, May 13, 1895.

"The Pearl and Gazelle to be Disposed of at Public Auction. Seized by the Marshal." Buffalo Enquirer, February 23,1895.

Buffalo Enquirer, February 25, 1895.

"Were not Sold." Buffalo Enquirer, March 6,1895.

Gazelle
Buffalo Morning Express, July 17, 1897.

"Drowned the Engineer. Yacht Glance Run Down by the Steamer Gazelle This Afternoon." Buffalo Evening News, September 28, 1897

"Death of Dilliot. Coroner Investigating the Sinking of Yacht Glance by the Steamer Gazelle." Buffalo Evening News, October 5, 1897.

"License Revoked. Inspectors of Steam Vessels Give Their Decision in the Glance Accident." Buffalo Evening News, November 3, 1897

"Gazelle Broke Down." Buffalo Express, August 10, 1898.

Buffalo Morning Express. June 22, 1899

"Accident to the Gazelle." Buffalo Express, August 25, 1900.

Puritan
"New Excursion Boat. The Puritan Successfully Launched at Mill's Yard Yesterday." Buffalo Express, May 21, 1893.

"Fire Badly Damages Puritan." Buffalo Courier, July 15, 1901.

"Fire on Puritan." Buffalo Express, July 15, 1901.

Buffalo Daily Courier, September 1, 1901.

"News of the Lakes. Buffalo Now Possesses one of the largest Tugs on the Lakes. Was Steamer Puritan." Buffalo Express, May 19, 1902.

State of New York
"A Gigantic Project. The Crystal Beach International Assembly." Buffalo Courier, June 6, 1895.

"The Opening Day. Inuguration of the International Assembly." Buffalo Courier, July 2, 1895.

Buffalo Enquirer, July 20, 1893.

"New Crystal Beach Boat Nearly Ready." Buffalo Evening News, Saturday, June 2, 1906.

"Mrs. Cassin, Barred at Gangplank, has Husband Arrested in Twinkling." Buffalo Courier, August 5, 1906.

A. J. Tymon
"On the Water. Thousands of Excursionists Carried to the Resorts in the Vicinity of Buffalo." Buffalo Express, July 5, 1894.

Advertisement. Buffalo Express, June 19, 1894.

Nellie
Buffalo Enquirer, October 30, 1894.

Buffalo Enquirer, August 7, 1894.

Garden City

Buffalo Morning Express, May 29, 1896.

Buffalo Evening News, Thursday, August 20, 1896.

Shrewsbury

"First Picnic of the Year." Buffalo Courier Record, May 16, 1897.

Marine Record, February 3, 1898. Maritime History of the Great Lakes, Walter Lewis. http://www.hhpl.on.ca/GreatLakes/HomePort.asp.

Superior

Buffalo Daily Courier July 30, 1901.

America

Buffalo Daily Courier July 20, 1901.

Lake Superior PORT CITIES. "What's Gone Down. The America: A Friend to North Shore Ports." Thomas Holden. Milwaukee County Public Library. Great Lakes Marine Collection. Official Number: Official Number: 107367.

Buffalo Daily Courier July 22, 1901.

Lincoln/Premier

Buffalo Evening News, March 11, 1904.

Buffalo Evening News, April 6, 1904.

Buffalo Evening News, April 8, 1905.

"New Boat on the Crystal Beach Line." Buffalo Evening News, August 6, 1906.

Buffalo Daily Courier, July 2, 1907.

Arundell

Buffalo Morning Express, August 1, 1878.

Cleveland Herald, Saturday, May 28, 1881

Great Lakes and Seaway Shipping http://www.boatnerd.com/

Buffalo Daily Times, May 5, 1905.

"Slight Damage to the Arundell." Buffalo Evening News, June 30, 1908.

Idlewild

"Launch of a New Steamer." Detroit Post & Tribune, Sunday, May 4, 1879.

"Steamer Idlewild Went Aground in Canadian Channel." Buffalo Evening News, August 7, 1904.

"Rudderless: 200 Aboard." New York Times, August 16, 1905.

Darius Cole

Port Huron Daily Times, July 16, 1885.

Port Huron Daily Times, October 5, 1885.

"News of the Lakes. Darius Cole the best excursion boat seen here in recent years." Buffalo Express, June 7, 1902.

"Moonlight Excursion." Buffalo Express, June 17, 1902.

"Drowned in Collision." Buffalo Express, August 21, 1903.

Buffalo Evening News, July 29, 1905.

Mascotte

Buffalo Commercial Advertiser August 1, 1887.

Buffalo Commercial Advertiser, August 5, 1887.

Buffalo Evening News, May 2, 1904.

Urania

Buffalo Evening News, May 2, 1904.

The Marine Review June 8, 1899.

Buffalo Morning Express, March 29, 1905.

Loss Reported of American Vessels, Merchant Vessel List, U. S., 1913.

Marine Review and Merchant Vessel List from Maritime History of the Great Lakes, Walter Lewis. http://www.hhpl.on.ca/GreatLakes/HomePort.asp

White Star
Buffalo Dauily Courier August 5, 1901.

"Struggle at Beach to Board Crippled Vessel; Women and Tots Suffer." Buffalo Courier, June 4, 1906.

"Disabled Crystal Beach Boat Repaired." Buffalo Courier, June 5, 1906.

Buffalo Daily Courier July 30, 1901.

Argyle
Ship of the Month No. 19. Empress Of India. The Scanner. Monthly News Bulliten of the Toronto Marine Historical Society. Vol. 4, No. 5, Feb 1972. John N. Bascom, editor.

"Sad Accident at Galt: A Pleasure Steamboat Goes Over The Mill Dam." Meaford Monitor, May 31, 1878.

"Over a Damn: A Pleasure Steamer Lost With Eighteen Persons On Board." Cleveland Herald, May 23, 1878.

Buffalo Morning Express, June 28, 1907.

The Scanner, Meaford Monitor, and the Cleveland Herald from Maritime History of the Great Lakes, Walter Lewis. http://www.hhpl.on.ca/GreatLakes/HomePort.asp

CHAPTER 3:
Others on the Run
"Steel Passenger Vessel Red Hot as Tug Arrive." Sandusky Register, September 1, 1925.

Pilgrim
"The Excursion Boats. As Business grows Perhaps the Boats will be of Better Class." Buffalo Courier, August 19, 1891.

Lake and River Resorts. Buffalo Express, May 8, 1893.

"Excursion Season. Some Wild-cat Trips Already Made." Buffalo Express, May 7, 1894.

Buffalo Daily Courier, June 6, 1894..

"Big Combination. New Company to Control Excursion Traffic." Buffalo Express, May 17. 1896.

State of Ohio
"A Gigantic Project. The Crystal Beach International Assembly." Buffalo Courier, June 6, 1895.

City of Erie
Valli, Isacco A. "The Great Race." Anchor News, March/April 1983.

"Three Boats to Crystal Beach on Saturday." Buffalo Express, August 6, 1908.

Anchor News from Milwaukee Public Library, Ship Information and data Record. Official No.: 127242.

Eldorado
Buffalo Enquirer October 8, 1892

Buffalo Enquirer August 14, 1893

Columbia
Buffalo Courier, June 22, 1894.

The Marine Review, May 4, 1899. Maritime History of the Great Lakes, Walter Lewis. http://www.hhpl.on.ca/GreatLakes/HomePort.asp

CHAPTER 4:

Americana

"Another New Boat for Crystal Beach." Buffalo Evening News, June 16, 1908.

"Excursion Steamer Americana Opens Crystal Beach Season." Buffalo Express, May 30, 1908

"Crystal Beach. Many Improvements Will be Observed There When the Season Opends." Buffalo Commercial, March 28, 1907.

"Crystal Beach Boat Launched." Buffalo Commercial, February. 22, 1908.

"Great Throng Sees Launching of 'Americana'." Buffalo Courier, February 23, 1908.

"New Americana a True Clipper." Buffalo Express, May 28, 1908.

"Steamer Americana Shows Her Paces." Buffalo Evening News, May 18, 1908.

"Two Rescued by Steamer in Midlake." Buffalo Courier, July 7, 1913.

"Boats Unable to Tie Up at Beach Docks." Buffalo Morning Express, June 1, 1926.

Inland Seas, Winter 1963, p. 322

"Canadiana's Skipper Glad To Have Permanent Home." Buffalo Courier Express, July 6, 1930.

"Americana Wins 36-Day Fight With Gales in North Atlantic." Buffalo Evening News, December 24, 1929.

"Steamer is Freed." Buffalo Cpurier Express, July 12, 1938.

"Captain of Americana, Former Buffalo Steamer, is Suspended." Buffalo Courier Express, August 7, 1944.

Inland Seas courtesy of the Lower Lakes Marine Historical Society, Buffalo, New York.

Canadiana

"Americana II. Crystal Beach Company Will Duplicate Steamer Now in Service." September 1, 1909.

"Canadiana. That is Name of New Crystal Beach Steamer Launched Today." Buffalo Commercial Advisor, March 5, 1910.

"Navigation is Opened." Buffalo Evening News, April 11, 1910

"Trial Trip of Canadiana Pleases All on Board." Buffalo express, June 12, 1910.

"New Steamer on Old Erie." Buffalo Express, July 1, 1910.

"New Crystal Beach Boat is on Exhibition this Evening.." Buffalo Express, June 30, 1910.

"Canadiana Sailing May 26 to Mark Opening of Beach." Buffalo Evening News, May 19, 1951.

S.S. Canadiana Preservation Society, Inc. Unpublished Manuscript, 1995-1997.

"Girl Leaps From Beach Steamer." Buffalo Evening News, August 1, 1929.

"Drowned Girl Identified." Buffalo Evening News, "August, 9, 1929.

"Woman Saved After Fall Off Steamer Deck." Buffalo Evening News, June 27, 1941.

"Pleasure Ban is Effective OPA Finds." Buffalo Courier Express, June 28, 1943.

"RCAF Pilot Crashes to Death in Lake Erie After Narrowly Missing Excursion Steamer." Buffalo Courier Express, June 20, 1943.

"Body of Young RCAF Pilot Recovered From Lake Erie." Buffalo Courier Express, June 21, 1943.

"Body of RCAF Flier in Crystal Beach Crash Recovered." Buffalo Evening News, June 21, 1943.

"Slot Machines On Ship Lure Minors' Coins." Buffalo Courier express, July 6, 1946.

"Opinion Asked On Steamer's Slot Machines." Buffalo Courier Express, August 10, 1946.

"Slot Machines on Boat Fall in City's Province." Buffalo Courier Express, August 16, 1946.

"Whirr of Coin Machines Missing on Beach Boat." Buffalo Courier Express, July 5, 1947.

No. 6 RCAF Museum, Dunnville, Ontario, Don Oatman, President.

"Couple, Cat Rescued from Stranded Boat." Buffalo Courier Express, September 2, 1951.

News reports on the riots can be found in Buffalo newspapers in May and June 1956. They are too numerous to list. Supplemental information about George C. Hall and the decision to discontinue operating the Canadiana from Harvey Holzworth, President of the S.S. Canadiana Preservation Society, Inc.

CHAPTER 5
Miss Buffalo II
"Dry Spell Ends for Crystal Beach Boat." Buffalo News, June 30, 1983.

"Big Band dancing Returns to Crystal." July 1, 1984.

"Comet Looks Forward to Backward Ride." Buffalo News, May 16, 1985.

Americana
"Americana Makes a First-Class Debut." Buffalo News, May 21, 1988.

"Crystal Beach Crowd Bused Home As River Rocks Disable Americana." August 25, 1988.

"Damage Sinks the Finale of Americana's Season." Buffalo Bews, September 1, 1988.

"Owner Seeks Fiscal Viability For Americana" Buffalo News, June 6, 1989.

Right: Buffalo's inner harbor circa 1920, with the twin steamers of the Crystal Beach Line - one approaching the Commercial Street dock, the other docked.

"Era to End With Sale of Americana Ferry Destined For Ports South." Buffalo News, July 4, 1991.

CHAPTER 6:
Mills Record, 047370. Marine Museum of the Great Lakes at Kingston, Canada.

"Cambria is Wrecked." Buffalo Evening News, July 28, 1897.

Mills Record, 009180. Marine Museum of the Great Lakes at Kingston, Canada.

"Crystal Beach Line. New Fleet of Excursion Steamers will be in Commission This Season." Buffalo Commercial, April 6, 1906.

"Fort Erie's Sesquicentennial Anniversaries and Milestones." Fort Erie Historical Museum, Ridgeway, Ontario. 2007.

CHAPTER 7:
"Canadiana's Engine Comes Home." Buffalo News, April 12, 2006.

"Canadiana Comes Up a Survivor." Buffalo News, May 7, 2007.

Index

Courtesy of Rick Doan